The Power of Failure

Developing Resilience in a Mad World

Author of the bestselling *Depressive Illness: The Curse of the Strong* (Sheldon Press), Dr Tim Cantopher studied at University College, London, and University College Hospital. He trained as a psychiatrist at St James' Hospital, Portsmouth, and St George's, University of London. He has been a member of the Royal College of Psychiatrists since 1983 and was elected fellow of the college in 1999. He worked as a consultant psychiatrist with the Priory Group of Hospitals from 1993 until his retirement from clinical practice in 2015. *The Power of Failure* is Dr Cantopher's seventh book: his other titles include *Toxic People: Dealing with dysfunctional relationships* (Sheldon Press, 2017), *Stress-Related Illness: Advice for people who give too much* (Sheldon Press, 2019) and *Overcoming Anxiety: Without fighting it* (Sheldon Press, 2019).

The Power of Failure
Developing Resilience in a Mad World

DR TIM CANTOPHER

First published by Sheldon Press in 2020
An imprint of John Murray Press
A division of Hodder & Stoughton Ltd
An Hachette UK company

2

A CIP catalogue record for this title is available from the British Library

Trade Paperback ISBN 9781847094834

eBook ISBN 9781847094841 (UK) / 9781529330939 (US)

Typeset by Cenveo® Publisher Services

Printed and bound in Great Britain by Clays Ltd, Elcograf S.p.A.

John Murray Press policy is to use papers that are natural, renewable and
recyclable products and made from wood grown in sustainable forests.
The logging and manufacturing processes are expected to conform to the
environmental regulations of the country of origin.

Sheldon Press
Carmelite House
50 Victoria Embankment
London EC4Y 0DZ

www.sheldonpress.co.uk

To Laura, who forgives my many failings.

Contents

Contents

Introduction

I'm a loser.

In fact, losing is one of the things I'm best at. I'm not bad at winning either, but though I say so myself, it's losing at which I excel. It's taken my whole life to get to this point, but developing the ability to lose really well has been worth all the time and effort. It's allowed me to be happier and to overachieve relative to my level of ability in the various fields of endeavour with which I've engaged over the years. I've managed to become comfortable with failing, which means there's really very little for me to be afraid of. I learn from my mistakes rather than punishing myself for them, and I'm able to take on things without knowing whether I'll succeed or not, which has made life a whole lot more interesting and has allowed me to expand my skill set steadily over the years.

It wasn't always that way. Until friends, colleagues and wise patients taught me the art of failing, it used to scare me so much that I avoided things which I wasn't sure I would succeed at. An example occurred on the beach at West Wittering, in West Sussex, when I was a young man in my early twenties. Friends had persuaded me to try windsurfing. I spent the day trying to stay on the board and to get it to move forward, with little or no success. Occasionally I fell into the water, but mostly I failed to get out of it in the first place. Exhausted and dispirited, I commiserated with another beginner who had enjoyed even less success and had endured even more hilarity from his friends than I had. 'That was awful,' I moaned. 'I'm not doing that again – it's impossible. I saw you were having a tough time, too.' 'It was great, hilarious. I really enjoyed it,' he replied. 'But you didn't manage to stay on the board.' 'I know, but I nearly did. Maybe next time.'

True to my word, I never did try windsurfing again. I did return to that beach, though, one sunny weekend day about a year later. As I strolled along the beach, I spotted the same young man with whom I had shared such a singular lack of success the previous summer. He was standing tall atop a board skimming the waves, turning nimbly and proceeding equally fast in the opposite direction, pausing only to leap in the air while waving at his friends. How had the clumsy oaf of a year ago become this expert of the waves? Hmm. Who had avoided repeated failure and humiliation? Who, on the other hand, had achieved mastery of a skill which brought such evident joy? Hmm.

The thing is that I had been taught to avoid failure at all costs. There were various sources of this learning, but the worst was my junior school maths master. By chance my year's intake had within it an unusual number of kids gifted in mathematics. In its wisdom, the school authorities decided to enable this cohort of bright children to realize their potential by putting them in the care of a teacher who was a retired army colonel. This ferocious man's bristling menace held us in a state of constant fear. The idea was, I suppose, that he would push us to greater heights than could be achieved by ordinary methods. One of his favourite strategies was to give us a really difficult maths problem to work through within a time limit. When the time was up, it was pens down and he would demonstrate the perfect working through of the test on the blackboard. On three of the lines of this specimen solution he would draw an asterisk. His rule was that if you had made an error on one of these lines, this was categorized as a 'silly mistake' and you were required to put your hand up, whereupon he would take you out and beat you with a stick. At the end of the working through, he would perform an audit of two or three of the class of twenty. If this revealed that you had failed to acknowledge that you had made a 'silly mistake', you would be beaten much more severely. So do I admit my mistake, with the painful and humiliating consequences which will follow, or hide it and risk something even worse?

The point of this unpleasant story is this: to my best knowledge not one of that class of talented kids went on to do a university degree in mathematics or physics. I'm fairly certain I know why. There's no more certain way of ensuring lack of success in any field of endeavour than by punishing failure. Contrast this with how really good teachers operate nowadays. They encourage, reward and use mistakes as an opportunity to learn. That doesn't mean that they welcome sloppiness or lack of effort, just that they recognize that if a student is stretched she will get some things wrong and that correcting those errors with patience and kindness is how her enthusiasm and abilities can best be enhanced.

One of the most inspiring examples of this principle of pursuing what you choose rather than avoiding failure was provided by my friend Jeremy Vine. Jeremy, as many will know, is a highly accomplished broadcaster. He is also a lovely man, as kind, generous and fun in person as he is in his public persona. Impressive though his many achievements are, in my view the most important is the video he put on YouTube during his run as a contestant on the TV show *Strictly Come Dancing*. This video post was in response to a troll who had complained that Jeremy was a bad dancer and who advised that he should withdraw from the show. With characteristic candour Jeremy thanked the correspondent and agreed that he had little talent as a dancer, but he insisted that he would stay on the show for as long as he was allowed to. 'If I gave up just because I can't be the best, what sort of a message would that give to my daughters? Should they avoid everything at which they can't win? No, I believe that we shouldn't just do what we're good at; we should attempt what is difficult for us and try to get better. I'm going to keep trying.' Now, if that's not courage and wisdom, I don't know what is.

The aim of this book is to help you to get more joy from life, to become more resilient and to achieve more. If you are a confident and optimistic person who treats yourself kindly, you need read no further. But most people tend towards self-doubt, excessive self-criticism and pessimism, and this book is for them. If that includes you, there are ways you can lead life more rewardingly and a good start is learning how to stop fearing and avoiding failure. My maths teacher was wrong, and I became liberated when I rejected his values. Jeremy and the windsurfer were right, and their lives are the richer for it. Follow their examples and you will become happier, less anxious and more accomplished. I can't claim that I've made exclusively great decisions in my life, but I'm happy because I've both forgiven myself for my mistakes and learned from them. I hope that you can, too. Life is a lot more fun and more productive if you don't beat yourself up.

There's more to resilience than befriending failure, though I believe that to be the most important skill you need. In this book you'll learn what makes people vulnerable to the challenges life brings, what qualities and skills protect against these challenges, and how you and those you care about can develop them. You'll see that there are some recurring themes. If you notice that something comes up more than once, you can take it that I think it's really important and worth dwelling on.

If you want some help with how to become happier, healthier and more resilient, read on.

1

Vulnerability and resilience

Why do some people suffer from stress-related illnesses and not others, given that most of us experience ups and downs in our lives? What makes one person vulnerable and another resilient? I've sort of started at the end, as having read the introduction you'll know that my view is that the biggest factor in this is the ability to fail well. But it's quite circular in that to be resilient to the reverses life throws at you, you have to be good at failing, while at the same time it's much easier to absorb failure if you're resilient in the first place. So there are clearly other factors which lie behind a person's resilience or vulnerability, and that's what we'll start looking at in this chapter.

First, we need to define what we mean by vulnerability and resilience. They can be seen as the opposite ends of a continuum determining how effectively we manage threats, challenges, adversity, changes and situations for which we are unprepared or ill equipped. Vulnerability is revealed by inability to cope and a tendency to be mentally or physically harmed when your environment is hostile, while resilience allows you to manage and to emerge relatively unscathed.

An alternative view of vulnerability is given by Dr Brené Brown. If you subscribe to Netflix, look up her lecture entitled 'The Call to Courage', which at the time of writing is on its list. It's an inspiring and entertaining talk. Alternatively, read her book *Daring Greatly*. Dr Brown sees vulnerability as an essential component of courage. The courageous person allows herself to be vulnerable. Vicky tells her boyfriend of three months that she loves him, because she sees that there's nothing to be gained by staying safe and reticent. Simon replies coldly and noncommittally. Vicky feels humiliated. She has bared her soul only to be rebuffed. But by putting her courage on the line, by allowing herself to be vulnerable, Vicky gave herself a chance of something life changing and good happening. It didn't, not this time, but that's not down to Vicky. If she does this again in the future whenever the odds are in her favour, she'll find happiness in the end. The humiliating rejection was in fact a triumph. Simon's response was, in the long run, irrelevant. It turns out that he's not the right person for her. But Vicky is courageous enough to be vulnerable, so her future is secure.

I'm going to use my concept of vulnerability for the time being, while nodding respectfully at Dr Brown and pledging to return to her work later in the book.

Genes

It's not that genes aren't important. Of course, what you inherit from your biological parents has an influence on your resilience, but it's not as much as you might think. Back in the 1970s a famous psychologist, Hans Jürgen Eysenck, stated: 'Everything in psychology is determined one-third by genetics and two-thirds by environment.' By environment he meant every influence throughout your life which isn't inherited. I haven't heard anyone in the field seriously challenge that statement since. So, if your parents and grandparents tended to be vulnerable to stress, you may be more at risk yourself, but there are many more important factors at play and there's plenty you can do to reduce your vulnerability. Don't blame it on your genes, as that leads you to give up. Above all, don't ever give up.

Personality

I've often heard people say of someone, 'There's nothing he can do about it, it's just his personality.' I say, 'Piffle!' You can change your personality any time you like, by changing the way you act. After all, what is personality? You define it by a person's behaviours. If you say someone has an outgoing personality, you mean that they go out a lot and interact with others. If a person has a generous personality, they often engage in generous acts.

I'll come back to how to change the habitual way you act later in the book, but for now I'd like you to put the concept of personality to one side. It's not rigid or immutable, so it's best to focus elsewhere, on our surroundings, resources, actions and thoughts.

Early life experiences

A baby is a blank computer hard drive. Childhood is about loading the programs and apps. They're pretty much loaded by the time you're 18. You can be affected long term by experiences in adulthood, but it takes a lot for them to have a long-term effect, while just about anything influences the way a child sees the world and copes with it. In order to mess up an adult who has enjoyed a consistently nurturing childhood, you really need to torture him or subject him to major life events or ongoing difficulties. For a child, however, all you need to do is to fail to be predictable, rewarding and consistently loving.

Parenting is hard, though fortunately you don't have to be perfect. In fact, there is evidence that parents who are 'good enough' bring up kids who are better placed to deal with life than those who are 'perfect'. That is, if your kids know that you love them no matter what, that they are important just for being them, it's OK for you occasionally to sit them in front of the TV while you have a rest. It's OK for you occasionally to be a bit irritable, so long as you later acknowledge this and effectively separate out for them what was justified chastisement and what was you being grumpy. It's OK for you to have your limitations. In fact, it's better that way, because that's the way the real world works. If your children learn in childhood that 'I'm OK and, though things and people aren't always good and happy, the world is OK, too', then all will be well. In fact, that's better than if you're always perfectly patient, loving and selfless, because sure as heck that's not the world they will emerge into when they leave home.

Consistently negative or inconsistent experiences in childhood do have an effect on how a child grows up. In fact, there's evidence that toxic influences even before birth can have detrimental long-term effects. Even accounting for the fact that mothers who have mood or stress problems in pregnancy are more likely to continue to have problems through the next 18 years, maternal anxiety and depression before childbirth predict stress-related illness in offspring to a greater extent than would be expected. For this reason, it does seem particularly important that anxiety and depression in pregnancy are effectively treated.

But it's childhood experiences that I'm mainly concerned about here. In particular, a child needs to learn cause and effect. If I do good stuff, good things happen to me – predictably. The opposite doesn't work; as I've already explained, punishment doesn't work. But what matters is that a child learns that she has control over what happens in her world.

Sarah doesn't learn this consistently. She is an only child four years old and (excuse the gender stereotype which is only to illustrate this example) spends weekdays at home with her mum while her dad is out at work. One day she asks her mum to set her up with her box of watercolour paints and some paper. She has been beautifully behaved all morning, helpful, quiet and polite, so Mum willingly does so. Sarah spends the afternoon preparing a painting for her dad. She puts her all into it, so when the time for her dad to come home from work approaches she's filled with pleasurable anticipation. She hears his key in the lock of the front door, so she rushes to greet her father.

4

'Daddy, Daddy, look what I've done for you. It's a painting, it's really good, isn't it? I did it for you, Daddy!'

But Daddy has had a bad day at work and is tired and grumpy. He stopped off at the pub on the way home and had a few pints of beer to drown his sorrows. The last thing he needs now is a screaming kid pressing paper covered in wet paint onto his clean suit.

'Get off, give me some space,' he growls, shoving his daughter aside as he stomps up the stairs to have a lie down. Sarah stumbles and falls to the floor, landing on the picture she had so lovingly prepared, which lies crumpled together with her hopes and expectations.

The next day Sarah is a nightmare to her mum, disobedient, demanding and oppositional. As she waits for her father to return she starts to worry that he'll be cross with her for being bad. But he has been feeling guilty all day for his grumpiness yesterday, so he has bought her a teddy bear and some sweets which he gives her as he enters the house, together with a big hug:

'I love you so much, you're the best little girl in the world,' he tells her.

Now Sarah, while being relieved, is confused. Yesterday I was really good and Daddy was horrible to me. Today I was really bad and he was nice, gave me stuff and told me he loved me. What's going on?

If these are isolated incidents that's one thing, but if life goes on like this, with no link between Sarah's actions and what follows, she will learn that she has no influence on the world, being helpless in the face of random and chaotic events. As a result she'll start giving up. What's the point in putting effort into things when the world is totally random. It doesn't matter what I do, she thinks, sometimes good things will happen and sometimes bad things; nothing I do makes a difference. This learned helplessness makes Sarah increasingly vulnerable, because her withdrawal from challenges, effort, social contact and anything else demanding makes her less able to learn skills, gain confidence or build a meaningful life.

Another mechanism by which childhood adversity leads to increased vulnerability throughout life is hormonal. Like all higher primates our body's response to stress is mediated by a chain of structures at the top of which is a part of the brain called the hypothalamus. This is linked by a bundle of nerve fibres to a small gland sitting just underneath the brain called the pituitary. In response to activation by the hypothalamus, the pituitary produces releasing hormones which pass into the blood stream. They act on two other glands, one sitting on top of each kidney, called the adrenals, causing them to release their hormones, in particular two which control our responses to stress, adrenaline and cortisol. The presence of these hormones in the blood in turn is detected by the hypothalamus, creating a feedback circuit. It is this circuit which determines our response to stress. Adrenaline is the short-term stress hormone, effectively gearing you up for a fight to the death by increasing heart rate, breathing, blood pressure, sensitivity of nerve endings and the pattern of blood flow around the body. Blood is pumped to the muscles and away from the surface of the body, allowing you to run faster and fight more effectively while not bleeding so profusely from superficial injuries. This is the fight-or-flight response. Adrenaline gives you the best chance possible of surviving an encounter with a sabre-toothed tiger or an enemy armed with a spear. The fact that the modern world contains few such hazards means that the adrenaline response is more often an unpleasant inconvenience than an effective survival mechanism.

The same is true of cortisol, which is the body's long-term stress hormone. This causes inflammatory processes and metabolism to slow down and the person (or animal) to be less active. In natural selection terms this again makes sense. In the face of a short-term threat, an animal needs to fight or escape effectively, while if the threat persists the animal will probably be injured or facing an un-survivable environment and will need to withdraw to a safe place to enable it to survive. In lower primates this is hibernation. In humans it is depression.

OK, I know this is a bit long-winded, but it comes down to this: the hypothalamic–pituitary–adrenal (HPA) circuit (or axis) is, like the brain, programmed through childhood. If a child faces adversity through the first decade and a half of life, she will develop an HPA axis which is super-sensitive, leading through life to a tendency to fight-or-flight responses and the longer-term effects of stress in response to lower levels of stress than would cause such reactions in others. In other words, childhood adversity makes her more vulnerable.

In fact, the HPA axis can be reset through adulthood, too; it just takes a greater degree of trauma or adversity. A child's brain is easier to influence. The other part of the brain which is programmed through life in this way is the pleasure/reward centre of the brain (a structure called the nucleus accumbens). Two chemicals in this structure, dopamine and oxytocin, mediate feelings of pleasure and allow actions and events to be experienced as rewarding. Prolonged or severe adverse events, especially early in life, reduce the levels of these chemicals in the pleasure/reward centre, making it more difficult for a person to enjoy things and feel good in the future.

Finally, there is loss. You would have thought that loss early in life would toughen a child up, but in fact the opposite is true. Paula copes wonderfully well at the age of 13 when her father dies suddenly of a heart attack. She is well behaved, doesn't cry and supports her mother. Everyone remarks on how well she has adjusted to the loss of her dad. Fast-forward 20 years. Paula now has two children of her own, a baby and a four-year-old. There are rumours of redundancies at work, and she fears she might lose her job. Then her mother, who provided child care for her, falls and fractures her hip, meaning Paula needs to make other arrangements urgently for her kids. She falls into a deep depressive illness. Why? How come this tough and resilient child became a vulnerable adult? The answer is resonance. Obviously, loss of your job or of childcare support isn't the same as the death of your father, but symbolically there is a link. All of them involve a loss of certainty, a sense of the world being safe and dependable and of you being securely at the centre of it. Paula suffers the double whammy of her current threatened loss resonating with past loss. Early loss leads to greater vulnerability later in life when the current loss, or threat of it, resonates with that suffered in childhood.

Life events, ongoing difficulties and social supports

A lot of research has been done on what in a person's environment puts him at risk of developing an illness such as major depression or a severe anxiety disorder. The results mostly aren't altogether surprising, though a few are. Major changes in life ('life events'), particularly those involving loss, are a major risk. That includes loss of a loved one through death or divorce, loss of a job, loss of financial security and anything leading to major loss of self-esteem. Even changes in routine which most would see as welcome turn out to pose a risk, such as vacations, promotions and major gambling wins (winning the lottery, for instance).

Interestingly, more toxic than any of these, at least for women, is having three or more children under the age of five at home. One remarkable study attempted to interview every woman in Camberwell, an inner London suburb, to look at what social factors predicted illness. Those who had three children in this age range without social supports had a greater than 50 per cent chance of suffering from a severe depressive illness. Any major ongoing difficulty is a risk, such as chronic illness, poor housing, long-term financial difficulties and problems with neighbours.

What comes across clearly in all the research is that isolation increases your risk, while consistent social supports are very protective. Supportive friends and relations keep you well. The trouble is that when you most need them, following divorce and after the first few months following bereavement, people tend to avoid you. It's one of the saddest and most consistent observations from bereaved patients of mine (and I do see divorce as a bereavement) that for the first few weeks after their loss, everyone is wanting to give them support and condolences. This is a period during which many are in a state of detachment, feeling very little and unable to benefit from all the attention. Typically, after a few months to a year or so, the enormity of their loss sinks in and the grief really bites. By then people have scattered and those willing to talk will tell them that they should be 'getting over it'. No, they shouldn't. You never get over grief; you just get freedom over time to feel it when you choose to, rather than being disabled by it all the time or being punched in the gut by it at the most inopportune moments. Life is never the same, but you do get a texture back, with happiness and other emotions occasionally providing contrast to the times of sadness and loneliness.

If someone you care about has suffered a major life event, particularly involving loss, is suffering ongoing difficulties or is isolated from supports, ask them what they need rather than pressing your solutions and advice on them. The ability to listen is usually a lot more helpful to a friend in need than is your homespun wisdom or your efforts to cheer them up. I'll come back to this point later in the book.

How you think

About 40 years ago the psychologist Aaron T. Beck described the thinking style of people who went on to develop major depressive illness, which he called the 'negative cognitive triad'. His work has been validated many times since. The triad comprises a consistently negative view of yourself, the world and the future. These thoughts are automatic and apparently uncontrollable. It's not difficult to see how self-defeating these thinking patterns are, and most people who have this way of viewing life do try to be more positive. But negative thinking is tenacious because it is based on deeply held underlying assumptions. Thoughts like 'There's no point in me applying for this job – things will never go my way, there will be lots of better candidates and the system is stacked against people like me anyway' are based on deep-seated underlying assumptions. If we were to dig persistently enough, we'd probably find these are along the lines of 'I'm no good, the world is aligned against me and my future is hopeless'. So you don't try for the job, fearing how badly you'll feel if you try for it and don't get it. Why would you feel so badly if failing to land the job only confirms what you knew anyway? Now that's interesting and something we can work on. The fact is that there's a little bit of yourself that feels you could get the job and you fear having this tiny spark of hope and positivity extinguished. That's what you're avoiding by not applying for the job. Then you can say to yourself and others, 'I could have done that job, but the system didn't give me a chance.'

The other factor perpetuating your negative and self-defeating thinking is the 'halo effect'. This is illustrated by the line in the Simon and Garfunkel song 'The Boxer': '... still a man hears what he wants to hear and disregards the rest.' In other words, we make up our mind about things, people and situations fairly early on and then fit the facts into our preconceived construct. If you feel good about yourself, you see achievements as the natural consequence of your merit, while reverses are just pebbles on your path to the top. Conversely, if you have Beck's negative cognitive triad, you'll focus on your failures as confirmation of your uselessness, while seeing any successes as fleeting exceptions which prove the rule that you're always going to come up short in the end.

An understanding of this is the basis of cognitive behavioural therapy (CBT), to which I'll return in Chapter 9. Your thoughts and underlying assumptions aren't set in tablets of stone; they can be changed.

Of all the predictors of stress-related illness, the most powerful is your *locus of control*. This describes how you see the way your life is controlled. Do you merely react to what the world throws at you, or do you take steps to organize your environment the way you need it to be? Joe suffers with anxiety and tends to avoid things and situations which scare him. He feels powerless in the face of an unpredictable and frightening world. He feels only as good as the last thing he has managed to do, and as he avoids most things, he feels bad most of the time. Even more than this, he feels only as good as the last thing someone said about him. He craves affirmation and praise, but he rarely gets it. He is essentially a cork on the ocean, briefly up when good things are said about him or happen to him, but down when the world turns hostile, as it so often does. He has no control over the world; it controls him. He has an external locus of control.

Phil, in contrast, recognizes that he faces a lot of challenges which he's not well placed to overcome, so he determines that he needs to change things. He's become a bit isolated, so he makes himself go out more. He calls up old friends to re-establish contact so that he has more supports. A girl who he would like to date is keen on heavy-metal music, so he downloads some of this music in order to be able to talk to her with some knowledge of this genre. Phil is doing what he can to alter his environment, to make it work better for him. He has control over his world. He has an internal locus of control. The most powerful thing you can do to become more resilient is to shift your locus of control internally. Again, more on this later.

I'm going to talk a lot about *mindfulness* later, but it needs a brief mention here. This is the ability to experience life in the present on its own terms. A mindful person is fully aware of everything around her. She avoids projecting into a hypothetical future, or ruminating about the past unless she needs to in order to make a plan or to learn from her mistakes. As soon as she's able to, she returns to the present and attends to who and what surrounds her. She avoids fighting unless it is unavoidable, and accepts what is and can't be changed.

Mindfulness isn't yet one of my strengths, though I'm getting better. I have had a tendency to dwell on mistakes and unfairnesses in the past, while quickly glossing over my achievements and good fortune as another bullet dodged and to be forgotten. If I let myself, I tend to catastrophize, as if by imagining the worst possible outcome I'll somehow prevent it from happening. This isn't a confessional; I'm quite proud of the progress I've made over the years in becoming more mindful, but I'm still working on it.

Are you mindful? Test yourself on this from time to time. A simple test I gave my patients was: 'What colour are the flowers outside the main entrance to the building I'm seeing you in?' Many were unable to answer, because they had been wrapped up in thoughts about what they were going to say and ask me in the forthcoming session. I would tell them that's a shame, as the appointment arrives in its own time, while the flowers were what was available to them then. Try something like this yourself. Describe the details of the place you passed half an hour ago, then go back and check how accurate you were. Or some variant on that theme. If you're not very mindful, work on this – it'll be worth it. I'll give you some more hints in this area later.

I'm not going to go into psychoanalytical models of vulnerability here. That's not to say they aren't relevant, but in my experience fewer therapists use these models to inform their therapy than used to be the case. However, modern ways of looking at concepts such as the ego are a bit easier to turn into concrete advice. Freud and those who followed in his footsteps described the ego as being the central concept of self – how you see and experience being you. A fragile ego meant you would be vulnerable because everyday events would threaten its integrity.

The more modern concept which I turn to is 'OKness'. If you know that you're OK, it's very difficult for people or events to demoralize you. I knew that I wasn't the greatest psychiatrist in the world. I trained with some of them. They had immense intelligence, encyclopaedic knowledge, enormous empathy and bucket loads of charm. They had gorgeous partners and spouses and usually had a golf handicap of 1. I can't claim that I never felt any resentment or envy towards these folks, but at the end of the day I could cope with their excellence and good fortune because I knew that I was OK. I was in my view worth my fee and was better at my job than many. This sense of OKness gave me a lot of protection through the ups and downs of my career. From time to time folks would tell me that I was wonderful, the best psychiatrist in existence. While I welcomed flattery of this kind, it didn't alter significantly my view of myself. I'm OK. At other times, for a variety of reasons, I would face virulent criticism, suggesting I should give up and let someone more competent take over. These events upset me, but not for more than a few hours, because I knew that I was OK. While being totally insulated from others' feedback and criticism makes you arrogant and ignorant (who said 'Donald Trump'? That's a scurrilous slander!), a solid sense of OKness at your core is a powerful source of resilience. It's well worth looking for.

People

In my career I learned fairly early on that the stressor which causes people to get ill most often is other people. While good relationships make you resilient and while they lead to most

13

of the joy available to you in life, dysfunctional relationships cause the greatest pain and make you the most vulnerable. One of life's many ironies is that it's only good people who are messed up by toxic ones. If you are insensitive, self-centred, lazy or hard-nosed, a cruel or manipulative person can try as hard as he likes, he won't be able to hurt you. But if you're one of life's givers, diligent, sensitive and selfless, it's a cinch for him to bully you and bend you to his will, particularly if you lack confidence in your own worth. Some toxic people develop very sharp antennae and can spot someone they can use and abuse from a mile off. If you wonder why you find you are surrounded by people who only make demands of you and never give you anything, that's the reason. They don't waste their time with people who have solid self-esteem and firm boundaries, because they are harder to manipulate. There are lots of good people out there; most people are quite nice most of the time, though we all have our moments. But good people hang back and wait to be asked. They don't press themselves on you and so they get crowded out by the takers, who will always muscle their way to the front of the queue for your affections.

I need to touch briefly on the subject of *gameplaying* here. In this context, games are not fun recreational pastimes, far from it. The concept comes from the field of transactional analysis, and specifically from one of its founders, Eric Berne, author of the book *Games People Play*. I recommend this book. While it's over 50 years old, it's a classic, easy to read, instructive and admirably short. Berne describes games as covert interactions designed to place the victim of the game in a position which he would not voluntarily occupy. The player does this in order to achieve a reward (the 'payoff').

Berne gives a lot of examples, but I'll give one here. I'm tired and irritable after a tough day at work. I've had to keep up a calm, therapeutic and professional facade at work, and by the time I get home I'm ready to pop. If I declared to my wife that

I wanted an argument to let off steam, she'd conclude that I've become stranger than ever and wouldn't take me seriously. So I say nothing and just grunt when she greets me. 'Are you OK?' she asks. 'Yes, I'm fine,' I snap back. I then sink into sullen silence, punctuated by occasional sighs. After half an hour of this she can take no more and says, 'Oh, for goodness' sake, what's the matter?', to which I reply: 'Well, I've had a rotten day at work, not that it seems you're interested; you haven't even asked me about my day.' Now, while my wife is a wonderful person, she isn't a canonized saint, which you'd have to be not to fire back something short and angry. So there it is, my payoff: the argument I've been looking for, following which I feel relieved while my wife feels upset and tricked, which she has been.

Almost every relationship has very occasional games in it of one kind or another. While annoying, that isn't a big problem. But if your whole relationship, having lost the spontaneity and intimacy which it once had, is based on a series of games, you are going to become increasingly vulnerable. Gameplaying as a way of life does great harm and over time makes the victim ill. *Unless* she finds an *antithesis*, which is a manoeuvre which prevents the player gaining the payoff. There's more on this in Chapter 7.

If you want to look more deeply into people who can harm you, read my book *Toxic People: Dealing with Dysfunctional Relationships*. For now, just recognize that your kindness and generosity, if not accompanied by firm boundaries, may be fine attributes, but they may also make you vulnerable.

Shame

Many of us have been taught that shame is a valuable emotion, an indicator from God, society or yourself that you're doing wrong. I don't agree. There is a large body of research showing that shame is a destructive emotion which does few people any good. It would be one thing if habitual miscreants felt shame and therefore changed their ways. But they don't. Far from feeling ashamed about their misdeeds, they tend to be proud of them. They look not for approval or respect but for opportunity. Politicians, in my view, should be ashamed of themselves quite often. As you are all too aware, they aren't. On the contrary, they seem to be proud of themselves, particularly when they have been shown to have lacked honesty.

At the other end of the spectrum are people who are plagued by shame. Many of them found their way to my consulting room, and were suffering from anxiety, depression or addictions. I rarely found that their shame did them any good. Far from enabling change, shame kept them trapped. Let's take Eric as an example. He suffers disabling social anxiety and starts drinking to control his nerves, and because he's ashamed that he's not more confident. Inevitably, while alcohol helps him overcome his anxiety in the short term, over a longer period it makes it worse. Now he has three problems, his anxiety, his problem drinking and his shame. He suffers even more shame, and it takes even more booze to cover this over. While he's drunk he feels nothing, but when he's sober his shame is crushing. And so the spiral into addiction starts. If Eric is going to have any chance of overcoming his addiction, he's going to have to deal with his shame first. In any case, his shame is ill founded; anyone can fall into the trap of addiction – what defines a person is not whether they have had problems or made mistakes, but what they then do about it.

So there's another of life's ironies. Those who should be ashamed of themselves aren't, but those who shouldn't be are. It's a funny old world ...

Diet and habits

There is a lot of literature on this subject, so I will touch on it only very briefly here. Yes, diet does matter, but don't believe those enthusiasts who try to persuade you that all life's troubles and ailments are caused by what you eat, or that going on their patented diet (at a special discounted offer if you sign up today for a gazillion pounds) will solve all your problems. The truth, like in so many aspects of life, is about balance. A balanced diet and a lifestyle in which there is balance between the various priorities are how you can be as resilient as possible: not too much caffeine or alcohol, regular moderate exercise (it is possible to take too much exercise), limits on work, time for rest, regular meals comprising a balanced diet and getting enough sleep – all this is well known and important in building resilience.

Coping strategies

I will outline specific coping strategies which are effective later on. For this chapter the only point I need to make is that you need some. That's not as obvious as it sounds. Many of my patients had no coping strategies at all, other than pleasing people and trying increasingly hard. They careered through life without any direction or purpose. Life is a rocky path, and however carefully you plan your route and pick your steps, you're going to stumble. Then what? You can just plough on or you can re-evaluate and find a better route. If you are stumbling a lot, if your life is going nowhere, stop for a while and look at what skills you can learn which will help you to navigate your life better in the future.

iGen

The sociologist Jean Twenge named the generation which was born recently enough never to have known life without a smartphone 'iGen'. You'll find the details of her work in the bibliography section at the end of this book. In essence, she concludes that this generation is more vulnerable than previous ones because of their dependence on social media. In my day bullying was a fairly straightforward affair. You did what the bigger boy wanted or you got thumped. It's much more compli-cated now. An iGen kid has to get her fair share of Facebook likes and Twitter followers or her mood and self-esteem plummet. Balance in life is much harder to achieve when academic and social requirements compete with social media for space and importance. Bullying can be so much more effective when the smartphone ensures there is no escape from it.

The bottom line is that suicide, major depression and severe anxiety are all becoming more prevalent in young adults. Changes in how society works caused by the internet and social media seem to be a major factor in this.

So that's a quick trip through some of the factors which make us resilient or vulnerable to the stuff life throws at us. Next, I'll look at two qualities whose influence on how effectively we manage challenges is so big that they deserve their own chapter.

2

Optimism and happiness

Your ability to cope with life is so profoundly influenced by your ability to be optimistic and happy that I've given these qualities their own chapter. Of course there is again a circular relationship between resilience, optimism and happiness, but we need to start at the point which can be changed. You can change your level of optimism and become happier by changing what you do, what you choose and how you think, as we'll discuss later, so it's worth studying these qualities carefully.

Optimism

There has been a lot of research done on optimism and pessimism, and I'll summarize some of it here. Optimism and pessimism form a continuum in any population – a graph plotting the levels of optimism versus numbers of people shows the familiar bell-shaped curve that applies to most traits (Figure 2.1). This graph shows that we aren't divided into optimists or pessimists, but that each person has a place on this continuum, being more or less optimistic. I will talk about 'optimists' and 'pessimists' for brevity, but be aware that when I do I'm really referring to arbitrary points on this graph.

The research does suggest that most people maintain roughly the same place on this graph throughout life. Once an optimist always an optimist, and vice versa. But it doesn't have to be that way. The genetic effect on optimism is fairly small, accounting for about 25 per cent of your level on the graph. Childhood experiences, as described in the last chapter, are bigger factors,

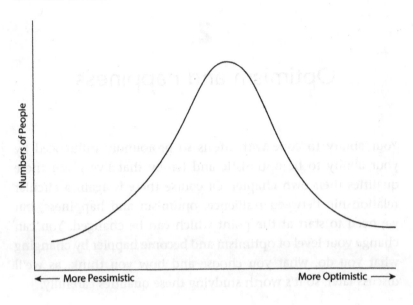

Figure 2.1 Level of optimism/pessimism in a population

but most important of all are the ways you think and act – and these you can change.

A large part of your wellbeing is whether you have clear goals. In my view, these should be kept as simple as possible, so you know what you really want in life. Many years ago I sat myself down and decided what I really wanted, which I was able to boil down to a list of three: to love and be loved (OK, I know that's strictly two things, but cut me some slack here), to make a bit of a difference to some people with what I do ('a bit' is the crucial part here – I'm not talking about curing all illness), and to get a single-figure golf handicap. Through the years I knew what I was aiming for and that helped me a lot.

Two aspects seem to be important when dealing with goals: the value you place on them and your confidence in being able to achieve them. A person who places a high value on her goals and is confident of ultimate success will persevere through the ups and downs she faces along the way and thus will enjoy a high chance of realizing them. A person who doesn't care much about her goals, hasn't properly worked out what they are or has little confidence she can achieve them will be likely to give up at the first challenge she faces. In this context, optimism is confidence pertaining to life in general.

So how come some people who have had bad things happen to them remain optimistic? The answer lies in framing. Optimists frame an adverse event as a one-off, not predicting anything for the future and not personal to them. In contrast, pessimists conclude that since some bad things have happened, they always will and they feel plagued by bad luck, which attaches to them like a leech. Their world is framed by the misfortune which they experienced in the past.

Moving up the graph in Figure 2.1, from pessimism to optimism, is very important because so much good in your life flows directly from you being optimistic. Faced with problems, optimists search for solutions while pessimists, expecting the worst whatever they do, experience anxiety, anger, sadness, or even despair and depression, resulting in them giving up. Optimists are happier much of the time and get more out of life because they engage more. Do optimists, expecting a positive outcome from whatever they undertake, set themselves up for disappointment? It seems not, because when something he takes on goes pear-shaped, an optimist labels the failure as a temporary reverse and a useful learning experience on the path to success.

The concept of coping is important here. It's not so much the good things in life which determine whether or not we thrive, as how we cope with the bad, annoying or stressful things. Optimists cope by engaging with problems and trying to overcome them. When it turns out that a problem can't be completely solved, they tend to find ways of reducing the damage, either practically or emotionally. That is, an optimist faces an insoluble situation and tries to avoid it bringing him to his knees. For example, facing a cancer diagnosis, an optimist will accept the reality of his situation, placing it in as positive a light as is realistically possible, determining to fight his disease with everything at his and his doctors' disposal and using humour from time to time to break the gloom. In contrast, a pessimist will delay going to his doctor until his symptoms are disabling, will deny his diagnosis for as long as he can, then give up, isolate himself and wait for death when he can't avoid the reality of his illness anymore. So the fact that optimists tend to accept adverse situations faster than pessimists doesn't mean they give in to them; quite the opposite – to deal with a situation effectively, you first have to accept it.

Optimists expect good things to happen, but they don't sit and wait for them. They take actions which make them more likely. They make their own luck. For example, an optimist expects good health, but she exercises regularly, eats well, doesn't misuse alcohol, drugs or tobacco, and takes medical advice, which makes good health very likely. She takes appropriate action if she suffers unexpected symptoms, but she doesn't routinely scan for symptoms or signs of illness. Pessimists tend to spend a lot of time scanning their bodies for signs of serious illness and worrying about any symptoms which they may develop. They tend to be slow to get professional advice as they fear what they may be told and tend to avoid things which remind them of their worries. They take little exercise as they feel that their future is bleak whatever they try to do to stay healthy. If they feel overwhelmed, they tend to retreat to alcohol or drugs to gain temporary relief from their fears, resulting in further deterioration in their health.

As I explained in Chapter 1, stress leads to changes in the body, in particular release of the hormones adrenaline and cortisol, and if levels of these chemicals remain elevated in the long term, adverse physical effects ensue. However, there is good evidence that optimists are less reactive than pessimists to stress, with lower circulating levels of the stress hormones to a given level of trauma or threat. As a result, facing a stressful lifestyle or ongoing difficulties, optimists are at much lower risk than pessimists of developing stress-related illness, either physical or mental.

Beyond merely good health, optimists enjoy better lives anyway. High scores on measures of optimism at age 18 have been found strongly to predict higher income ten years later. Optimists tend to be more popular, with larger social networks and more supports (all being important to wellbeing) than pessimists. You may have spotted that there could be a circular effect here, with popularity, good supports and high income likely to make you more optimistic, as well as the other way round. However, even when this is taken into account in research, it is clear that developing a more optimistic outlook leads to more and improved social relationships and more satisfaction in those which you have. In addition, optimists work harder at relationships and are better at resolving problems and conflicts in them than are pessimists.

So, in summary, becoming more optimistic confers a host of potential benefits as well as enabling you both to overcome problems and to better endure those which can't be overcome.

Is there a downside to optimism? It's difficult to find one, though there may be a slightly greater risk of an optimist developing a problem with gambling or engaging in reckless behaviours such as driving too fast. Expecting that luck will turn your way and a big win is just around the corner is a sure way of getting into serious debt, and overtaking on a corner because you assume your luck will preserve you will end with you in A&E. I hope it's not too controversial here to bring up evangelical Christianity. I live in a place where it is the norm, and many of my evangelical acquaintances deny the reality of climate change on the grounds that 'God will protect us'. This sort of optimism is a threat to us all. So optimism doesn't do away with a need for caution and prudence; it just makes it more likely that you will be happy and healthy.

Do optimists always persevere in the face of adversity? No. In fact, when it becomes clear that a task cannot be successfully completed, optimists give up more quickly than pessimists and start looking for an alternative task at which they can succeed. Joyce is unhappy in her job working the tills and stacking shelves in a supermarket. She wants to be elevated to a supervisor role, but her manager, who has been at the store forever and took against her from day one, has told her she won't get the promotion. Being a pessimist, Joyce assumes that if she tried to get a better job elsewhere she would fail, so she stays put and tries to change her manager's mind. But the manager is stubborn and inflexible, so Joyce can't succeed and so becomes increasingly frustrated and miserable. Joyce's colleague Abby, on the other hand, while having less experience and fewer qualifications, is having none of it. Having been given the same brush-off by their manager, Abby immediately looks for another job. She's an optimist, so she expects it all to work out and isn't going to keep banging her head against a brick wall where she is. After several unsuccessful interviews Abby eventually gets a great job as a management trainee in a competitor store the other side of town.

Optimism works. You can become more optimistic, and you can find out how later in this book.

Happiness

I've already indicated that one key to being happy is becoming more optimistic. But there's more to it than that. There's a lot which goes into making a person happy, and a great deal of research has gone into the subject, some of which I'll summarize here.

Happiness is about going beyond surviving, coping and achieving. It's about thriving and flourishing. In order to understand this, it's useful to see a person as existing on two axes, *mood* and *arousal* (level of alertness). A person with low mood and low arousal is depressed; a person with low mood and high arousal is anxious; a person with high mood and low arousal is calm, while a person with high mood and high arousal is enthusiastic, as shown in Figure 2.2.

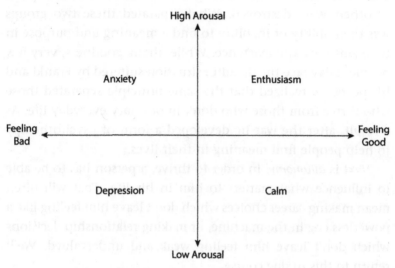

Figure 2.2 Mood and arousal

To be happy you need generally to have a fairly high level of mood but also to be able to move your level of arousal from lower to higher as appropriate to your situation. When we come to discussing how to become more resilient, we'll be looking at how to get happier, and that in turn will mean looking at how to improve your day-to-day mood and to control your level of arousal.

Central to happiness is finding *meaning* in your life. This may be through family, work, religion, art, sport or a host of other things, but whatever it is, it needs to give you a meaning and purpose for being alive. You need to feel of value, whether or not others acknowledge that value. The Jewish psychologist

Viktor Frankl was imprisoned in a German concentration camp during the Second World War. He survived the Holocaust and went on to write a book, *Man's Search for Meaning*, based on his experiences and observations during that awful time. His essential finding was that some of those who escaped the gas chambers survived the ordeal relatively intact while the spirits of others were destroyed. What separated these two groups was their ability or inability to find a meaning and purpose in their suffering and existence. While, thank goodness, very few people today face the dreadful situation suffered by Frankl and his peers, he realized that the same principle separated those who thrive from those who don't in ordinary everyday life. As a result, after the war he developed a form of psychotherapy to help people find meaning in their lives.

Next is *autonomy*. In order to thrive, a person has to be able to influence what matters to him in his life. That will often mean making career choices which don't leave him feeling like a powerless cog in the machine, or making relationship decisions which don't leave him feeling weak and undervalued. We'll return to this in due course.

Then comes *aspiration*. A happy person has something to aim for and look forward to, a focus for her efforts. She has hope that things will get (even) better, because she's working towards a cherished goal. That said, the goal has to be achievable. She has to believe that she has, or has a chance of developing, the competence to carry it off. Zoe has an ambition to study part-time with the goal of achieving a business degree so that she can apply for a management position. She will need a supportive boss who allows her half a day a week to attend the course and a source of financial support to cover her tuition costs. She will also need to believe that she has the intelligence and application to have a chance of success. If her boss is unsupportive, she may have to consider looking for another job, which means taking a risk, as her current post is fairly undemanding and well paid and has generous perks. So what sounds simple for Zoe – getting happier – turns out to be a bit more complex than it seemed.

It is possible to be a happy hermit. People at the far end of the scale of introversion can do it, but in practice I've met very few people who are happy in isolation. It's a lot easier to be happy through positive interactions and *relationships* with others. The most important of these will, of course, be with your spouse or long-term partner. *Love* may not conquer all, but it sure does lead to a lot of happiness or sadness.

You need energy to get happy. Mostly, happiness doesn't get visited upon you; it requires you to go and find it. So *vitality* is a necessary factor in happiness. This implies trying to be as physically fit and healthy as possible, but also running your life in balance, so there are time and resources available in your effort to find happiness. I'll come back to the importance of balance shortly.

Variety, so they say, is the spice of life. This is backed up by research showing that having some variety, texture, change and even a bit of unpredictability in your life increases your chance of being happy. A boring and predictable job, if combined with a humdrum home life and a week dominated by routine, may be reassuring, but it rarely leads to long-term happiness.

Clarity is another important factor. This is particularly important at work, where the happiness of a workforce is as dependent on the clarity of their objectives and the required steps to achieve them as it is on the terms and conditions or remuneration of their jobs.

It's a lot easier to be happy if you feel respected. Having a *valued social position* (status) is an obvious source of happiness, but performing any role which you and at least one other being (human or animal) see as of value will do it. So being a carer of an elderly parent can lead to happiness, even though the role may seem isolating and thankless. I've seen some very happy individuals who have little contact with anyone other than their pets. Being part of a group with value either to society (e.g. a soldier in the army) or to its members (e.g. a member of a football supporters club) can make you happy.

Support is one of the most important components of stable happiness. This may come from any direction: family, friends, colleagues, church (and God) or just the guys down the pub. Happiness means having somewhere to turn when you're in need.

Can *money* buy you happiness? I'd like to say no, and to an extent I can, but it is undeniable that both long-term unhappiness and depressive illness are much more common in areas of deprivation and low income/high unemployment.

I also need to list one feature which you might think is central to happiness but isn't. *Fairness*. Life isn't fair and it never was. I've not met one happy person who looks for fairness. The truth is that from time to time life will fail to reward you for your effort, diligence, merit or virtue, and may even kick you in the teeth for good measure. But at other times it will present you with a bouquet which you haven't earned.

Physical security is important for happiness, but to a degree which varies a great deal from person to person. I doubt there were many happy people in the trenches of the Somme, but some members of the armed forces whom I have met actually valued and even enjoyed the physical danger they faced. A totally safe life devoid of any risk or uncertainty is a happy one for very few.

Which brings us back to the issue of *balance*. For many of the features and circumstances I've listed, you can have too much of a good thing, as illustrated by the graph in Figure 2.3.

For example, variety implies change. Too much change introduced too rapidly leads to stress, reduced performance and unhappiness. Likewise, while contact with people is important, too crowded an environment in which there is no possibility of

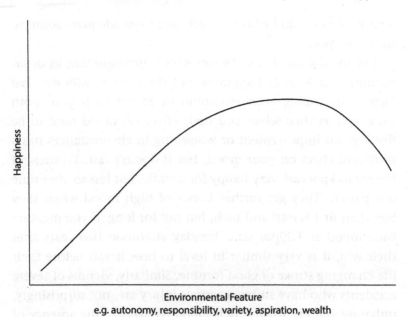

Environmental Feature
e.g. autonomy, responsibility, variety, aspiration, wealth

Figure 2.3 Environmental features versus happiness

alone time is harmful to wellbeing. Too high a social position can weigh you down with excessive responsibility. Too much aspiration in the face of factors resisting your progress can lead to disillusionment and demoralization. There is even evidence that there is a level of wealth which is optimal for happiness, above which fear of losing it all takes over. I once had a patient who became severely depressed when his accountant informed him that his personal wealth had fallen below £100 million. Everything is relative.

So what is needed in your life is balance, not abundance. Where this tipping point lies for each of the factors I've listed depends on the balance between them. For example, you can overcome a challenge of greater severity and complexity when you have more control, autonomy and support. So in your sales job you can sell more units and enjoy the job more if you are allowed to be involved in developing the strategy, have flexibility over your hours and who to target, and have adequate administrative support.

I've listed a number of factors which are important in determining your level of happiness, but these are mostly external factors, describing your environment rather than you. Both these factors themselves and their effect on mood tend to be fleeting. An improvement or worsening in circumstances has a profound effect on your mood, but it doesn't last. Winners of lottery jackpots are very happy for a while, but less so after time has passed. They get further bursts of high mood when they buy their first Ferrari and such, but not for long. If you measure their mood at 3.30pm on a Tuesday afternoon two years after their win, it is very similar in level to how it was before their life-changing stroke of good fortune. Similarly, victims of severe accidents who have suffered serious injury are, not surprisingly, unhappy, but eventually their mood recovers in the absence of other ongoing problems (such as financial or legal difficulties). A neutral event can be experienced as very pleasant or unpleasant depending on how it contrasts with what prevailed beforehand. So a plain meal of cornflakes and milk may induce great joy in someone who has been trekking across the desert for a month. A period of solitude about which previously he would have felt neutral may be experienced as very painful for a bachelor who has spent the last two weeks in the company of his new love.

So events affect your level of happiness, but only temporarily. It seems that we all have a personal level of equilibrium in our mood. Relying on a constant stream of positive events to shore this up is unlikely to be successful. Shifting the point of equilibrium will require us to look elsewhere.

Personal factors, relating to how you think and operate, are at least as important as the external factors I've listed. These include your personality, but remember that personality isn't static; it can change. Your sensitivity to stress, extroversion/introversion, conscientiousness, level of self-esteem and perfectionism (see Chapter 3) are all relevant, as is your level of optimism, as we've already established. How these personality traits affect your level of happiness depends on your circumstances. If, for example, you are a member of a supportive and high-functioning team at work, your conscientiousness is likely to lead to greater happiness. If, on the other hand, you have a lazy, manipulative, disengaged and unsupportive boss, your conscientiousness may make you miserable.

Your gender is also a factor. It is a sad fact (in my opinion) that married men are on average happier than their single peers, while married women are on average less happy than those who have never been betrothed. I'm not saying that women shouldn't marry, but there is possibly a point to be made in this context about social roles in marriage.

Probably the most important factor in determining your level of happiness is how you think. For example, comparative value judgements about the past, future and yourself are powerful determinants of happiness. Judgements like 'I expected it to be better' or 'It's only going to get worse' make you unhappy, while ones such as 'I dodged a bullet – it could have been so much worse' and 'It'll probably get better; this too shall pass' make you happier. Judgements about direction of travel, such as 'I'm making progress', are important. Hope that you will succeed in what you value is crucial.

Most powerful of all are comparisons you make between yourself and others. It's very difficult to avoid these judgements and their effect on happiness. For example, in a study of Olympic medalists, bronze medal winners were on average happier than those who won silver. The former tended to be able to value the fact that their achievement brought a tangible (and displayable) result, whereas the latter tended to feel 'I was so close, just a little more and I could have been Olympic champion'.

As a general rule, people who make fewer value judge-ments, especially about themselves and particularly involving the word 'should', tend to be happier than those who judge as a way of life. Happiest of all are those who spend most of their time experiencing the present rather than fighting with life, rummaging around in the past or fantasizing about the future.

Those who have read others of my books will be familiar with the statement 'You become the way that you act'. A person who acts happy tends to become happy. Certainly, what we do is more important in the long run than how we feel about it and just as important as how we think. I won't go further into this now, but will return to it repeatedly later in the book.

Of all the ways of acting, *altruism* is possibly the most potent source of happiness, as I have witnessed repeatedly through my life. A good demonstration of this is provided by that excellent organization Alcoholics Anonymous. Once sober, AA members are expected to work the 12 steps of recovery. They are helped in this endeavour by a 'sponsor', that is a person of the same sex with at least two years of recovery under their belt who has worked all 12 steps. Gradually, with your sponsor's help, you work your way through the steps, eventually reaching step 12, which is helping others. That is the point at which you become a sponsor to one or more other people. This immensely valuable role is entirely without material reward and I have seen it confer great happiness on some who take it on.

That was a whistle-stop tour through two of the most important components of resilience. Next we'll deal with a factor which many would see as a virtue, but which I see as a handicap: perfectionism.

3

Perfectionism and the quest for certainty

Many of us are taught as children that perfectionism is a good thing, the mark of a trier, the only way of realizing your true potential. If that's what you were taught, your teachers were wrong. Many of us carry this conviction into adulthood. We talk with awe of people who have excelled, saying things like: 'Look at her achievements – she's wonderful, a real perfectionist.' No she isn't, she's just someone talented who has put a lot of work into getting as good as she can at what she does. That's very different. Perfectionism doesn't work; it's inefficient. The thing is that, like many specious ideas, perfectionism is nearly right. In order to achieve what you're capable of, you need to try hard, be persistent and give the enterprise your full attention. But that's not quite the same as seeking perfection. The psychologist Bob Rotella wrote a best-selling book entitled *Golf is Not a Game of Perfect*. The premise is that you can get as good as you are capable of being at golf by accepting that you will sometimes hit bad shots, accepting the consequences of those mistakes and keeping a positive focus on the next shot. Well, I've got news for you: life isn't a game of perfect either. Patience, persistence and realism are going to enable you to achieve a lot more than chasing the illusion of an error-free life.

Where does perfectionism lead? The answer is obvious, because perfection is impossible to maintain. It leads to failure. But hang on a minute, I spent the Introduction trying to persuade you that failure is a powerful friend, didn't I? Well, yes, I did and it would be if you could receive it that way. But if you're a perfectionist, you can't accept or tolerate coming up short, so with failure comes shame. I dealt with shame in Chapter 1, but I think it's worth returning to it briefly here. To summarize, shame is usually destructive, though many of my generation who were brought up strictly are prone to it. In practice, most people who do bad things on any regular basis don't feel guilt, because they're constitutionally unable to do so. They're able to rationalize their misdeeds as acceptable responses to their circumstances. They're good at minimizing the importance of their actions. They habitually project – that is, they take the worst aspects of themselves, place those characteristics on other people and then attack them for it. Larry realizes in his heart of hearts that he's lazy and doesn't pull his weight at work, so when his team loses a contract because the work hasn't been done, he blames Paul and goes around the company running him down. The alternative, which Larry won't countenance, is feeling ashamed. But what about Paul? If he's a good and diligent person, he may feel aggrieved for a while, but as part of him feels that he could have stayed even later at work and given up even more of his home life for the project, he'll sooner or later feel shame.

So where does this shame go? What effect does it have on Paul? Does he learn from it and modify his work pattern to become more efficient? No, he doesn't, because for someone who cares as deeply as Paul does, shame is intensely painful, a trauma. People tend to recoil from things which are linked to trauma, so Paul will tend to give up, to work less hard, less thoughtfully and less efficiently. I've met very few people who have the fortitude to learn from shame. For most, its effect is withdrawal and apathy.

Let's be clear: I'm not arguing against personal accountability, just about what it is. Accountability is a word beloved of politicians (who mostly refuse to take it themselves) and the press (which uses it mostly to attach blame to someone when misfortune happens). The word actually first came into common parlance in the 1960s when a new way of running businesses was proposed by experts at Harvard Business School. Previously, most organizations had been run top down, with the CEO telling his senior managers what to do, they in turn giving instructions to the department managers, who then gave specific orders to the workers on the shop floor. The new idea was to devolve responsibility down the chain of command. So rather than me telling you what to do, I give you an area to take care of yourself. You won't know exactly what to do as you don't have the experience which I as your manager have. That means you'll make some mistakes. That's OK, it's inevitable. The only requirement is that you admit your mistakes, discuss them and, with my supportive help, learn from them. That way, in a short period, the whole organization gains expertise, confidence and autonomy. Sadly, in modern Britain, this far-seeing concept has often been taken over and changed by those who want to find easy ways of feeling better by persecuting those who have made mistakes. The misuse of the concept of accountability makes good people vulnerable.

So what about *remorse*, which is valued and even required in many penal systems? Is it helpful? How is it different from shame? The answer is that it can be, with a lot of time and supportive help. Dave, who is guilty of a crime which has done harm to many people, may have difficulty understanding the gravity and consequences of his actions. If he is going to become a safe and useful member of the community in the future, he's going to need a lot of help gaining this understanding. He's not going to achieve this by being told repeatedly that he's a terrible person. It's not the whole person who needs to be condemned, but the action which caused the harm. If Dave can understand that he is more than his worst actions, he can start to shift his behaviours and attitudes. He can feel remorse for his crime because he can see that he's potentially a better person than that. So remorse attaches to an action and can lead to useful change, while shame relates to the whole person, is destructive and leads to withdrawal.

If you wonder why your friend can't accept your criticism, it may be that he feels you're attacking him rather than just criticizing his one action. And the lower a person's confidence, the more he will take a criticism of a single event as a personal attack on him. Conversely, the better a person starts to feel about herself, the more she can learn positive lessons from criticism and reverses.

Perfectionism leaves you very vulnerable to *scapegoating*. As a perfectionist you'll find yourself taking responsibility for most things, because nobody else will take the issues as seriously as you will. If you haven't read Tara Westover's brilliant but horrifying book *Educated*, I recommend you do so. It is an immensely brave account of her abusive upbringing in a survivalist family in the American Midwest. Her account describes her father as a bully with a mood disorder of some kind which made him unpredictable and reckless, a mother who chose to defer to her husband rather than to protect her daughter, and a sociopathic brother who horrifically abused her and other family members. When eventually Tara escaped this toxic family environment for long enough to understand its dysfunctionality and to call them on it, they turned on her. She became the scapegoat upon whom the family could pin all the blame, while hiding and denying their complicity in the years of neglect and abuse and the harm caused by them. Being someone who easily took responsibility for things, who was a perfectionist (she went from having no basic education to achieving a PhD at Trinity College, Cambridge), who tried very hard and who wanted above all the love of her family, she was an obvious candidate for scapegoating. The concept of the scapegoat is a very old one, going back to ancient Judaism, where at times of famine God would be appeased by the people's leaders selecting a goat to bear the sins of the whole community. This poor creature was then driven out into the desert to starve, with the sins of the population dying with it. Scapegoats are valuable in dysfunctional systems, whether they be families or other groups, allowing everyone to avoid accountability and to feel better. The cost is only to the scapegoat, who will become increasingly vulnerable as time goes on. Oh, and I guess also to everyone else, because nothing ever changes, hmm! 'Once abused always abused' is a rule of thumb which, while almost a cliché, tends to be true. People who have suffered abuse or neglect tend to go from one such relationship to another, because they have insufficient confidence or self-worth not to and because abusers are very good at finding vulnerable people to abuse.

Cognitive dissonance is another consequence of perfectionism. This is defined as the distance between your ideal self and your real self. Those of you who have read others of my books will recognize the guy in the cartoon in Figure 3.1 who turns up

Cognitive dissonance

Figure 3.1

in several of them. He's pumping weights because he wants to become big and strong in order to impress the girls and his friends. Ideally, he would like to be Mr Universe. The trouble is that he's a scrawny little chap and he has as much chance of realising his goal as I have of becoming Pope. But he's intelligent, charming and funny and is a pleasure to be around. If he focused on these strengths he could be a lot happier and more resilient, but this doesn't fit with his perfect vision of himself. His problems (and injuries) are largely self-inflicted, a result of his cognitive dissonance which in turn flows from his unrealistic perfectionism.

Perfectionism isn't just about you, of course. It also relates to your view of the world and the future. Life isn't perfect, it isn't safe, it isn't fair. Nothing is certain (other than, as Woody Allen says, death and taxes) and nothing (other than possibly love and faith) lasts forever. But a perfectionist has difficulty with this. She wants life to be right. She wants to be able to control

Figure 3.2

it, to stop things going wrong, to eliminate risk and suffering, to remove ambiguity, to find certainty in life. Well, good luck with that, but I fear it will end in tears. Trying to nail life down is like trying to nail down an armful of eels. You'll just make a mess and hurt yourself in the process. By all means take proper care over things and exercise proper caution in your judgements, but that's it. Focusing on the process works. Demanding of life that it then delivers the result you want doesn't.

I like pushing myself to do as well as I can at whatever endeavour I'm engaged in. But I'm not perfect in any way (I hear a resounding 'You certainly aren't!' from the unruly element at the back of the room), and I won't try to be. For me, being as good as I can sustain without causing myself or those around me any harm is better than perfect. As for the world, it'll carry on in its own rather odd way whatever my feelings about it are. Hey-ho.

4

Illness and recovery

All you really want is for everything to be good, everyone to get on and be happy, and for bad things not to happen. You wouldn't do anyone any harm, and you can be counted on in times of need. That's OK, right? Nobody could argue with your position. Well yes, I could actually. You see, I have a friend who's like you. Tom (not his real name) is such a kind man. He tries to fix everything and everyone, whether he's asked to do so or not. As often as not, the result of his unsolicited efforts is to make things worse. For example, when Andrew was ill, Tom corralled all his friends and neighbours to do shopping, cook food, mow the lawn, take in and collect the dry cleaning, and visit regularly to offer support. But neither Andrew nor his wife Mary wanted any of this. Mary just wanted to be left alone to deal with the practical and emotional fallout of her husband's illness, and to reach out for support as she needed it. The result of all this unwanted attention was that Mary became exhausted and irritable, culminating in her having a stand-up row with her best friend, Beryl, who had brought round a pie for their supper. This led to Beryl withdrawing, hurt and offended, meaning that Beryl's emotional support which Mary relied on was unavailable just at the time when it was most needed. The road to hell sometimes is paved with good intentions. Particularly if you don't listen to what the object of your efforts really needs.

But it's the harm done to you from trying too hard to do the undoable which is the biggest problem. Whether it's driven by perfectionism, fear of uncertainty, keenness to please or insufficiently firm boundaries, trying too hard for too long in an effort to make everything right leads, in order, to conflict, disillusionment, stress, reduced performance, then eventually illness. This is because the human body isn't designed for extended periods of running at 100 per cent of capacity. Essentially, natural selection has stopped because there aren't many things nowadays which kill you before childbearing age, which is what natural selection works on. So we're designed for life on the primordial plane, which was characterized mainly by occasional opportunities such as killing an antelope for food and crises such as being confronted by a sabre-toothed tiger. In those days, whether or not you passed on your genes was determined by how well you managed those brief episodes of opportunity or crisis. Nothing prepared our bodies for 12-hour days in a badly run office with a capricious boss, unrealistic targets and an ever-present threat of redundancy. Because those circumstances tend not to be immediately fatal, there is little natural selection advantage to learning how to pace yourself and set yourself realistic goals; hence we are poorly designed for a life of perpetual motion.

The end point of the journey for the person who tries to achieve perfect safety and certainty in an undermining environment is illness. In my career I saw more doctors suffering from stress-related illness than in any other profession. Police officers, nurses, firefighters, ambulance crew and teachers weren't far behind. What all these professions have in common is that they are directly or indirectly answerable to government. Each time a new government is elected, the new set of politicians (who as far as I can tell rarely suffer from stress-related illness – hmm) establish a fresh set of decision-making bodies, targets and bureaucratic structures. The hoops to be jumped through by general practitioners, whose jobs are tough enough anyway, get higher and higher and increasingly pointless. The cynics find a way of getting by, giving lip service to the new rules, pretending to follow them, looking good but mainly protecting their own comfort and welfare. The good, honest triers keep giving it their all until they break. When the going gets tough, the tough get ill.

Surviving as a good doctor is about risk management and pacing yourself, as well as all the other skills a physician needs. The same is true for anyone facing a stressful and demanding environment. Grappling head on with difficult challenges against insurmountable odds for too long leads to illness. This may come in a host of different bodily changes and diseases, many caused by the short-term adaptive changes which the body makes to deal with being under threat for too long.

Often, the first bodily system to crack is the gut. Stress leads to increased production of stomach acid and increased gut motility (the body's attempt to increase energy intake). The resulting inflammation of the stomach and intestines causes abdominal discomfort, bloating and/or symptoms of irritable bowel syndrome. Blood pressure and heart rate go up; blood sugar and fat levels are raised (fight-or-flight reaction), leading to increased risk of diabetes and heart disease; muscles go into spasm (ballistic muscles being in a state of contraction for too long); nerves become super-sensitive (adapting to perceived threat), manifesting as myriad aches and pains. These changes are unpleasant and alarming, leading to potentially disabling anxiety. Prolonged cortisol release triggers a hibernation response in the brain, experienced in humans (the cost of having developed a brain with a large emotional capacity) as major depression. The immune response is compromised, increasing vulnerability to infections and leading to a higher risk of developing cancer.

I want to avoid alarming you unnecessarily here. A short period of stress does you no harm, but the point I'm making is that struggling for years to achieve the undoable does.

So then what? You have been brought to a halt by stress-induced illness. For now you can't solve everyone's problems or keep everyone happy. You can't be the person everyone turns to; you're too sick. For once, others will need to do stuff for you, rather than the other way round. There will very likely be an issue here, as it's very unlikely that others will help you to the same extent you would help them if they were ill, but that's just the way it is. No point in being resentful about that – you don't reap what you sow because the world isn't built that way. Just because you give a lot of yourself to others doesn't mean that they are obliged to do the same for you.

But this is your *opportunity*. Your ailment can be the first in a long and grim line of illnesses, or it can be the blinding light on your road to Damascus (apologies to those of you who are not Christian – I mean your moment of clear insight). This is the time to reset and make choices. Your body is giving you a powerful message that it can't keep going like this. So what are you going to change? Are you going to keep going with your efforts to make life safe, to be certain things will go right, to keep everyone happy all the time? That's what got you ill, made your life a mess and led to people being cross with you. Or are you going to look for a better *balance*?

The issue of balance is the crucial one here. I'm not talking about changing everything, becoming self-centred or lazy. That sort of switch to the opposite of what you've done before doesn't work, because opposites are really not very different from each other. You'll end up switching from one extreme to the other with no real, sustained change occurring. Figure 4.1 illustrates my point.

The really radical move, one which can last, is to the centre ground. You will find the resilience which you want by lots of moderate changes. I'm going to go into more detail about what to change and how to go about it later on, but for now I only want to establish the point that your illness had causes, some of which are under your control and can be changed. In order to achieve that, you'll have to give something up, in particular

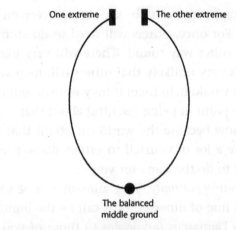

Figure 4.1 Extremes are not so different from one another

your role as the person who seeks perfection, keeps everything safe and makes sure everyone is happy. As horrible as stress-related illness is, it is, like failure, your friend and teacher if you'll stop and learn.

I'll give you an example. I have suffered from occasional attacks of migraine throughout my life, though far less often since I retired from clinical practice. When I was getting toward the end of my postgraduate training I was working at St George's Hospital in London. At the same time a team there was researching the outcomes of migraine sufferers. I've never seen the results of the study in print, so I can't back up what I learned from the researchers, but I found one of their preliminary findings very interesting. It was that if you suffer from migraine and when you have an attack you stop work and go to lie down in a darkened room, you have a significantly lower chance of death from heart disease or stroke than the general population. If, on the other hand, you suffer from migraine and battle through it, never taking time off to rest through an attack, you have a significantly *higher* chance of death from these causes than your non-migraine-suffering peers. It seems that, at least for some, migraine may be a flashing light metaphorically as well as literally, indicating that it's time to change your habits. Looking at it this way, migraine is a gift, an early warning system for those fortunate enough to have it and wise enough to take heed. My wife points out that I wasn't very good at taking heed or taking time off work, and so I count myself as fortunate to have reached the calmer waters of retirement relatively unscathed. Do as I say, not as I did!

Any illness affected by stress can be seen the same way – an indicator of a need for change.

5

Developing adaptability

We've spent enough time laying out the problems: why it is that some people are more resilient to stresses and reverses than others and what the main threats to our wellbeing are, at least those which we can control. That was the difficult part. Now for the easy bit, which is to work out the solutions – the changes which we can strive for that will make things better. Once you understand the problems, the solutions are obvious. I'll come back to my central points about failure and perfectionism later on, but in this chapter let's go back to the beginning of the book and work through what we can do about those factors which underpin vulnerability and resilience.

Genes and personality

You can't change your genes, more's the pity. But you can change your attitude towards them. The fact that your genes may predispose you to be vulnerable to stress simply means that you may need to do more work on getting good at managing stress than the next person. OK, so get started as soon as you've read this book. And though you've been assuming for years that you're stuck with your personality for life, you aren't. You can change not only how you seem to others but how you feel inside, because of the principle that you *become the way that you act*.

This is going to need some planning and strategy. Remember that opposites aren't real changes; they are just reactions to each other. For example, extreme dieting and overeating are just two sides of the same problematic relationship with food.

The radical change is to moderate healthy eating, with no punishing restriction and with occasional planned treats, not linked to mood (don't use food to deal with difficult feelings). Extreme overworking and inactive laziness are opposite sides of the same coin, which will tend to flip from one side to the other. The stable, sustainable change is to consistently try hard, but with boundaries. I could go on, but you get the point. If you want to change how you feel, you need to change how you act, *gradually*, moving towards the centre rather than swinging to the other extreme. Make a plan for what you're going to do differently and make sure it is realistic, not heroic. Maybe talk to a friend or someone sensible in your family and bounce your ideas off them.

Nigel, who works all hours and tends to be tetchy at home, wants to become more relaxed, less uptight. He'll need to start by cutting a few corners at work and at home – not becoming lazy but setting boundaries and seeking balance. He'll talk to his boss about his need for administrative support and for half a day to be set aside for admin. He'll talk to his wife about sharing more chores and seeking agreement on what doesn't need to be done perfectly or done at all. Then he'll look for things to add into his life which are fun, not serious, not goal-related, such as hobbies, sports and interests. He'll look at how his very relaxed friend Geoff runs his life and will copy some of what Geoff does. All of this feels alien and certainly doesn't make Nigel feel relaxed *to begin with*. In fact, asking for what he needs and wants makes him squirm. He'll feel guilty about not doing everything for everybody. But feeling uncomfortable is a good sign. For Nigel, because he's so diligent, *guilt is good*. Breaking the habits of a lifetime will always feel uncomfortable at first; that comes with the territory. Nigel needs to persist, avoiding any extremes. If he does, in time his more balanced and less driven lifestyle will become the norm and Nigel will begin to feel less overwrought and overwhelmed by life.

If you see yourself in Nigel, start to change the way you act; shift slowly towards the centre, not swinging to the other extreme. Look at people who are the way you'd like to be and start to copy them.

Early life experiences

What to do about a messed-up childhood? Remember Sarah from Chapter 1? She has developed learned helplessness because of inconsistent experiences in her early life. She avoids challenges and social contact and has largely given up, with no ambitions or aims. That's understandable, because she learned early on that she has no influence on what happens to her or around her.

What can Sarah do to turn things around? There's only one thing which is going to change the negative program which she has in her head: experiencing life as more rewarding of effort. Sarah needs to learn that you often get out of life what you put in. Not always; as I've established, life isn't always fair. Not immediately. So here we have a problem. I'm going to suggest that Sarah takes some emotional risks, that she puts herself out there, interacts more with people, takes on challenges. But then people are sometimes going to let her down. Sometimes she'll be unlucky and her efforts won't pay off because of bad breaks. This could confirm Sarah's view that life is random and that she has no influence on it. So other things are needed as well. Those things are reframing and taking a longer-term view.

Sarah applies for a job which she wants, even though she feels pessimistic of success. It's a great start. But she doesn't even get an interview. Now her learned helplessness could be confirmed, but it doesn't need to be. She needs to ask herself if there's another way of framing what happened. Maybe she could ask the personnel officer who posted the job what proportion of candidates got an interview and why she wasn't one of them. Perhaps she's told that only 10 per cent got an interview. Well, then, the odds were always going to be against her. They were looking for someone with experience or something in their CV which made them stand out. OK, it wasn't going to happen this time, but it was worth trying. Sarah has learned something about preparing her CV, too. Now she needs to keep looking and applying. The chances are that she'll be successful eventually by playing the numbers game. If she doesn't have a job after several months of trying, Sarah may need to rethink, but not until then. And while not being ruled by her feelings, she needs to recognize that they are hurt each time she doesn't get the job. She needs to look for someone sensible and supportive with whom to talk through her disappointment when she's unsuccessful and to keep it in proportion.

In summary, dealing with adverse early life experiences leading to learned helplessness or other vulnerabilities is about finding a way of being able to re-engage with life and then sticking at it long enough for good things to happen. Even more than that, it needs to be long enough for your HPA axis to be reset. Remember, this neurological and hormonal circuit is programmed easily in childhood, but is much more sluggish in responding to changed circumstances in adulthood. You're going to be more vulnerable to stresses than someone who has had an ideal childhood, at least for a while. That's why persistence is so important. I will look later on at other ways you can recalibrate your HPA axis, but for now the message is: *keep going*.

Parents, remember you don't have to be perfect; in fact, it's better if you're not. Just try to be as consistent and unconditionally loving as you can. The occasional slip-up is OK. If your daughter, now adult, suffers with anxiety, low self-esteem or signs of learned helplessness, don't beat yourself up about it. It happens sometimes even in the most nurturing families. But do encourage her to engage with the world, take some emotional risks, reframe her perceived failures and take a longer-term view. Make it clear that you value more the fact that she keeps trying than what the results of her efforts are.

Life events, ongoing difficulties and social supports

Major changes in life need to be taken seriously. While persistence is necessary to get what you want from life, so is flexibility. That means that when life punches you in the gut, you go down on one knee and take a breather before resuming the fight. Strength and courage need to be tempered with wisdom and care for yourself. There is a time for struggle, but also a time for sadness and licking your wounds. I know I'm mixing my metaphors here, but in the storm the stout oak falls while the bendy reed survives.

Figure 5.1

Remember that while adverse life events are the main threat to your wellbeing, even welcome ones can put you at risk if you soldier on too rigidly. A promotion at work, moving house or the birth of a child are all joyous events, but also a shock to the system, which needs to be taken into account. New parents will laugh when I advise them to take some time for themselves, for rest and recreation, but I'm serious. It is possible with good planning and a willingness to 'divide and conquer' and it's worth it.

Major ongoing difficulties are even more potentially toxic than one-off events, for obvious reasons. If you're an unmarried mother with three children under the age of five living in a tower block with no neighbourhood and with no family or close friends to support you, you're up against it. But in the absence of anyone else to care for you, at least you can care for yourself. It isn't possible to be a great parent under these circumstances, so just aim to be *good enough*, while leaving some time and space for yourself. It's not that you are more important than your kids, but you matter, too. If you go under, it won't be any good for them, so look after yourself first. This applies not just to mothers with small kids but to anyone facing protracted challenges in their life. And if there is any potential support available, go get it. It is a strength, not a weakness, to admit that you need help. Strangely, people like to be needed and will like you the more for reaching out to them. If they don't, then at least you know they aren't really friends and you don't need to waste any time on them in the future.

If someone you know asks for your time or support, please give it to him if you can, even if you're tired, busy and it's inconvenient, presuming he isn't one of life's habitual users (more on them later). There are certain times in your life which define you. Being reached out to by a person in need is one of them. Above all, though, don't give him unsolicited advice. This often makes things worse because your advice may be right for you, but as likely as not it won't be for him. If he feels under pressure to follow your well-meaning instructions, this will in all likelihood increase his distress. Listening and doing what is asked of you by someone facing major difficulties is much better than imposing your solutions on those who haven't asked for them.

How you think

Changing your habitual thinking patterns is probably both the hardest and the most powerful way of being happier and therefore more resilient. If you've always had a negative view of yourself, the world and the future, this is hardwired by now. But there's the difference between the electrical wiring of a communications network and that of the human brain. While the former is a static physical structure, the latter is fluid and adaptable. The longer your thoughts have followed one path, the longer it takes to change to a different path, but if you keep going, eventually you will.

The process of identifying your negative thinking patterns, digging further for the deep-seated underlying assumptions which generate them, challenging them and replacing them with more helpful assumptions and thoughts is the basis for cognitive behavioural therapy, of which more later (in Chapter 9). But you can start doing this now. Don't let yourself just feel bad without asking yourself: 'What am I thinking? Why? What is behind this? Is there another way of thinking about it? Is this alternative view more likely to be accurate? Then I'll go with it.'

Following the example in the 'How you think' section of Chapter 1, the answers would be:

> I'm thinking there's no point in me applying for this job for all the reasons I listed. Underlying are the beliefs that I'm no good, the world is against me and my future is hopeless. Another way of seeing it is that I really don't know what I'm capable of, the world is random and the future is unknown. That sounds plausible. OK, I'll apply for the job then – I've got nothing to lose and at least I'm doing something.

After you've applied for the job, this process continues. If you don't get the job, your negative thoughts will re-emerge and you'll need to repeat this process of thought-challenging. In fact, this process of challenging your habitual thinking patterns and underlying assumptions needs to become a continuous one, a new way of life. Your 'hardwiring' can be rewired, but only by a lot of repetition. Persistence is the key. I'll come back to this when discussing CBT, giving more detail on how to take this process forward, but for now just get into the habit of challenging the way you think.

When challenging your thinking, pay particular attention to the halo effect. Do you only focus on the negatives, the dangers and your failures, while ignoring and discounting the positive possibilities, your successes and examples of good fortune? Well then, challenge yourself, look for alternative narratives.

Work on your locus of control. This will need mainly to involve a change in the way you act. You're going to need to start putting yourself out there a bit more, taking some emotional risks. What you do at this stage is more important than how you feel about it. Your actions may seem bogus and pointless, but *do it anyway. Fake it to make it.* Joe from Chapter 1 needs to look at what Phil does and take some hints from him. He needs to start slowly engaging more with the things he is frightened of and which he has been avoiding. The results of Joe's efforts really don't matter at this stage; success will come along when it chooses to. What matters right now is that Joe starts doing some stuff rather than just avoiding things which scare him. He is starting to take charge of his world rather than having it be in charge of him. He is moving his locus of control internally.

I'll come to mindfulness later (see Chapter 9), but for now you can start trying to stay more in the present. When you find yourself wandering off into a hypothetical and catastrophic future, pull yourself back to the present and make sure you are really aware of and experiencing what is around you. Accept the things you can't change and fight only when you really have to.

Try to accept yourself and that you're OK. Not perfect, but perfect is no use anyway for reasons I've explained. By all means seek to improve, but be moderate and realistic in your aims. You're you and that's OK. This view of yourself can be very hard to achieve, so you may need help from loving friends or family. Talk to whoever is kind, warm and supportive about how you feel and *listen to* what they have to say. If they have nice things to say about you, this may make you squirm, but listen and register their words anyway. If you're isolated and there really is nobody who you can talk to in this depth, then imagine you are a close and loving friend of yourself. How would you talk to this person? Have this internal discussion with yourself.

Now I realize that if you're someone who has always lacked self-esteem, my words will sound hollow. My telling you to believe that you're OK is very different from you believing it. I know that, but OKness is so important that I urge you to search for it. Maybe you need to find what it is that you're passionate about; maybe you need to find what lies at the root of your poor view of yourself and seek to reframe it by talking it through with someone you trust. Do they see you the same way you see yourself? If you're Christian, maybe seek to reconnect a bit with your faith. If God loves you, it probably isn't right to hate yourself. If OKness is still elusive, don't despair – much of the rest of this book is aimed at developing it.

The truth is, I don't know exactly what is going to give you the realization that you're OK. But you do, if you think about it and talk about it with an open mind. This may mean dropping or at least setting aside for now your prejudices. You can't argue with prejudice; it's just prejudice. 'I'm a waste of space, always have been and always will be' is prejudice. It's not based on valid data. Nothing I can say will change your mind, because prejudice isn't open to rational argument. So do and think something else, as if you were OK, regardless of what you believe. If you need to, seek therapy. Your GP is your first port of call.

Dealing with shame

For the reasons I outlined in Chapters 1 and 3, if you are plagued by shame, the chances are that it's ill founded. Look at it critically. What are you ashamed of and why? You're ashamed that you're shy? That's a trait, not something deserving of shame. You're ashamed of your drinking? Anyone can fall into problem drinking, and many of the best people I've ever met are alcoholics in recovery. You're ashamed you're not better looking? Really? I don't think that even justifies a response. The things which you can't change need to be accepted. You deserve the same respect which you give to others, and a person's worth isn't defined by how they look or how confident they are. But you do need to look at what *action* you can take to try to change the things you can. You become more socially confident by having more social contact. In the words of a well-known book title, feel the fear and do it anyway. In the words of AA, fake it to make it. If you have a drink problem, get along to an AA meeting, or go and discuss it with your GP. Just don't sit and fester in your shame.

Whatever is the source of your shame, it can be challenged and brought under control, and if it's something which can be changed, there is action you can take.

Let's take a more difficult example. Say you've been convicted of a sexual offence. Now, having worked with a number of sexual offenders, I first split them into two groups: those who are ashamed and those who aren't. The latter group feel no shame because their offending arises out of a sociopathic (psychopathic) personality structure. Sociopaths are incapable of shame because they have no conscience. The former group is more interesting. Was their offending behaviour OK? Of course not. The more important question is how useful is the crushing shame they feel? The answer, beyond the period during which they were offending or immediately following their conviction, is that it's not useful at all. Shame tends to make you turn away from what needs to be done, to hide your head from the world. Putting shame aside doesn't mean refusing to take responsibility and be accountable for your actions. It means accepting that you are, like many others, a flawed human being who needs to try to change and improve. That's what is needed, action.

A sexual offender who manages, with help, to overcome his sexual addiction should in my view be proud of himself because he has achieved something which is both important and difficult. There is, of course, a difficult moral issue here: what about the person or persons who have been harmed by the offender's actions in the past? Does the offender not need to continue suffering in recognition of the harm which he has done? I can't satisfactorily answer that; I'll need to leave that issue to legal, spiritual and philosophical leaders to determine the issues of punishment and reparation. But the issue which I'm harping on is this: what works best? I can tell you for certain that for those who are suffering crushing shame which prevents them from taking action to improve things, what works best is to put aside their shame, roll up their sleeves and take action aimed at change.

Dealing with shame needs an enormous amount of honesty. You need to share your issues, warts and all, with at least one other person. Make sure they are kind and wise. Choosing the wrong person can lead to your problems becoming fuel for salacious tittle-tattle or to you being subjected to crass and ill-judged advice.

Diet and habits

I'm not going to spend much time on this here, but I include the issue for completeness. Balance is the key, with a healthy balanced diet, no fads, no trendy diets, regular meal times when possible, not too much caffeine or alcohol, and regular moderate exercise. There is very good evidence that those who exercise vigorously enough to get a bit out of breath and raise their heart rate above 100 beats per minute several times a week are less prone to stress-related illness than those who lead a sedentary lifestyle. Obviously, if you suffer with heart disease or other chronic illness, consult your doctor before attempting a five-mile run.

Balance is important in every area of your life: balance between work and rest, exercise and just hanging out, your needs and the needs of others, duty and having fun, doing things and sleep, I could go on and on. Balance in everything. No extremes, no heroism, just balance and persistence.

Electronic communication and social media

I'm not going to be able to persuade you to abandon Facebook and Twitter, though I eschew all this stuff and I don't think my life is any the poorer for it. But then I'm an old codger who doesn't face the same pressures to engage in social media as do the 'iGen' youngsters. But do recognize that in engaging with social media you are handling something potentially toxic. Young people who stop using their iPhones and other communication devices for six months become significantly less prone to anxiety and major depression, only for their rates of these illnesses to return to those of their peers when they resume their social media usage.

Once again, it's a question of balance. Make sure you have some time each day not spent on an electronic device. Talk to people regularly, particularly about the issues you encounter online. Never let yourself be isolated by the internet. If you are trolled, talk about it. Parents, you have a role here in imposing a sensible limit on time spent on devices, though I know how hard it is to put limits on a taciturn adolescent. Sometimes the role of the good parent is to be the bad guy. If so, embrace it.

Goals

In order to be happy and resilient, you need goals in your life. Keep them clear, simple and achievable. For me, three clearly defined goals in life are enough, but you can have one or two more if you want. If you don't have any goals, do some thinking. You need to find some. Remember that it's crucial that you care about your goals, that you value them highly and that you have some confidence that you can achieve them. That's why it's important that your goals are realistic. If you have no confidence that you can achieve anything which you value as worthwhile, then you're going to have to work on your self-esteem and your thinking style first. That may mean either getting some CBT, working with an online CBT programme or working through a CBT workbook (see Chapter 9).

Even before you do any CBT, you can start to challenge some of your assumptions and the way you think, as I indicated earlier in this chapter. Start challenging now the thoughts and assumptions which are stopping you from working towards your goals, or from even setting them.

I'll develop this theme in the next chapter, when I look at developing optimism and happiness.

6

Developing optimism and happiness

If you were super-confident and optimistic, might you frame the adverse events from your past and your bleak thoughts about the future differently? Yes? OK, so how about suspending your disbelief for a while and trying a different, more optimistic set of assumptions? Just try it and see where it leads.

Developing optimism

Even if it feels pointless, look for solutions to the problems you face. So what if it's pointless? It's better than wallowing in despair. Engage with the world even though you believe that your efforts are futile. When things go wrong, try framing them as temporary reverses, the first of two or more attempts which will eventually get you to where you want to be. If you don't believe it, just pretend for now and see where it takes you. Don't make a judgement the first time you come up short. This is a process. You've been withdrawing from the world and giving up on life for years. Now I'm asking you for just six months to try a different way of thinking and operating. Isn't that fair enough?

When something goes wrong, try to fix it if at all possible. If it really is unfixable, look for ways of reducing the damage, either damage caused by the event itself or the damage emotionally to you. For example, if you've inadvertently offended Michael, see if you can clarify that you meant no harm and make it up to him. If he's having none of it and won't even talk to you, try to reframe for yourself what happened: you slipped up, which all of us do from time to time, but it wasn't from malice.

You didn't do anything awful, you just said something which Michael took offence at; that's his choice. He could have sought clarification from you, but he chose to go off in a huff instead. Michael reacted extremely and quite meanly. Maybe you need to re-evaluate your friendship, or maybe you just need to wait until he's having a better day. At least you need to talk things through with someone you trust so that Michael doesn't continue to get under your skin and make you feel bad.

If a situation is bad and if you're powerless to influence it, try to accept it. Keep your eyes open in case anything changes. If an opportunity arises to improve things, take it. Always take action if there is action available. For example, if your doctor tells you that you've developed Type 2 diabetes, don't despair and wait to die. Take more exercise, lose weight, eat healthily, drink less, stop smoking, take more time for rest and recuperation. Many people who develop potentially serious illnesses become healthier than they have been for years by changing their lifestyle choices.

Limit the time you spend scanning. That means time scanning your body for signs of illness, scanning people for signs that they may not like you or may be upset with you, and scanning your environment for signs things may be going wrong. Obviously, some common sense is needed here. It's a good idea to scan the road before crossing it. Again, that word 'balance' comes up again. It's about taking appropriate action to be reasonably safe and to improve things when that's possible while accepting adversity and misfortune when it's not. And avoid alcohol or drugs as a way of escaping your pessimism. They may work in the short term, but there's no surer way of realizing your fears in the long term than dependence on substances.

As optimists enjoy better health than pessimists, you can use the circular relationship between your hormones and the stress you experience to your benefit. Working on your thinking by challenging your negative thoughts and learning to control your body's response to stress by getting good at a relaxation technique and mindfulness (see Chapter 9) will reduce the amount of adrenaline and cortisol your body releases. This will lead to you feeling less anxious and your mood lifting, which in turn will make it easier to be optimistic and therefore healthier, thus having less to worry about, and so on.

If you are facing a brick wall, don't keep pushing forward. In Chapter 2 Joyce sticks with her dead-end job because she assumes she won't be able to find anything better and she doesn't want to be disappointed. Abby does look for other opportunities and gets a better job. Whether or not you feel like Joyce, act like Abby. Welcome disappointment because it means that you've put yourself out there. Your reward will come eventually if you keep going.

As well as taking some emotional risks, record what comes of them. Keep a diary. If possible, share what you write in it with someone else who is more optimistic than you. They'll make sure that you record the results of your efforts fairly, rather than with a negative slant. And keep it in the present. You know what you're like, discounting anything good as a flash in the pan. 'Yes, I got this job; that was the only time I've been lucky in my whole life. It doesn't matter anyway as I'll probably be made redundant soon – last in first out.' No, stick to the present; you got this job. Put that in your diary together with how it makes you feel now, and then share your entry with your friend. The next time you're thinking of looking for a new job, reread today's diary entry.

If your pessimism is unshakable, go and ask your GP to refer you for CBT. It works.

I don't think it'll happen, but as you get used to being more optimistic, don't gamble. Assuming you'll beat the odds and consistently win at any game of chance isn't optimism, it's foolishness.

Getting happier

As I explained in Chapter 2, in order to be happy much of the time, you first need to learn how to control your level of *arousal*. You can't be constantly enthusiastic and excited or you'll exhaust yourself. You need to be able to be calm and content when you choose to be. That will mean getting good at relaxation and mindfulness.

To be happy, you need to find *meaning* in your life. That includes developing realizable goals as I explained earlier and working to develop the skills and confidence needed to achieve them. But it also involves finding meaning in what you've done and experienced in the past and what you're doing and experiencing now. I'll give you an example from my own life. Living now in the USA and having become a US citizen, I feel fully invested in my adopted country. But I face daily distress whenever our president (at the time of writing Donald Trump) or one of his tweets turns up on the news, because I find his persona disgusting and his views antithetical to everything I believe in. But despite this I'm happy. How come? Well, first because I see that I'm merely at a point in history which, like everything else, will move on. And my decision to live here, made before the 2016 presidential election, was a good one. It's sort of a privilege to be here to experience the bizarreness of it all. Second, it gives me something to fight for. I will do everything I can to ensure that someone better leads our nation as soon as possible. However small my part may be in the struggle to make the USA decent again, it's something. And third, in looking out for those who believe in the same things I do, I've met some really lovely people who enrich my life.

There's no need for you to become involved in politics, but you do need to find worthwhile meaning in your past, your present and your future. However difficult your circumstances may be, you can do this; just look at Viktor Frankl (Chapter 2).

He found meaning in living in a death camp. You can find meaning in your life, too. Think, search and talk until you find your meaning.

Look for *autonomy* if it is available. In order to be happy and resilient you need to feel you have some control over your life. Making bold career decisions in an attempt to find satisfaction in your work may be worth the risk. Powerlessness and pointlessness in your working life grinds you down. Is it worth it for financial security? The same question needs asking in relationships. Does your partner or your friend make you feel worthless and powerless? Is that a real friend? Is being alone for a while really worse than being used, undervalued and told what to do all the time? You don't necessarily need to abandon your relationship completely, particularly if you're married, but you need to fight for your space and to be treated with consideration and respect. Sometimes a bit of short-term conflict is the only way to carve out space for yourself in a relationship. Don't let yourself become isolated; sharing your problems with a friend and asking them for advice isn't disloyal. In the best relationships, both partners share things with friends outside the relationship too.

If you're an extrovert, your need for social contact is obvious. But what about if you're an introvert, shy and lacking in confidence? I'd love to tell you that it doesn't matter, but in truth most people need social contact to be happy. If you are genuinely content being on your own nearly all the time, that's one thing, but if the reason you're isolated is really a fear of social situations, that's quite another. It is worth dealing with your fear (or phobia) as that's the only route to happiness. The keys to achieving this are *systematic desensitization* and *reciprocal inhibition*. Systematic desensitization means slowly approaching the thing you fear (in this case people) in lots of very small steps, rather than one heroic leap. Reciprocal inhibition means you can't be both relaxed and anxious at the same time. So, to bring people and relationships into your life, start small and gradually work up the rungs of the ladder of your feared situations. For example, a start may be texting someone you know and arranging to meet for a coffee. Not lunch, not for long; 15 minutes is enough to start with. Each rung should only be a small step upward from what you've already managed. But before you even start, get good at a relaxation exercise (see Chapter 9 for one I recommend). Before any social task, do your relaxation exercise so that your anxiety is kept under control. When you're able to engage with people, which may take some time, take some risks. In particular, risk rejection. If you ask someone out and she or he says no, that's a triumph, not a failure. You faced your fear and put yourself out there. The result wasn't as important as the fact that you did it, because if you refuse to be daunted and keep trying, eventually someone will say yes.

Try to maximize your *vitality*. Get fitter if you can, lose weight if you need to, limit your alcohol and caffeine consumption, eat regularly and healthily, get sufficient sleep (that's different for every person, but you know how much you need) and then it's that word again: balance. Make sure there is enough balance in your life for you to have some energy left to enjoy life. Yes, I know that's really hard given the pressures of modern life, but if you recognize that *you matter too*, it is possible to give a bit more to yourself regardless of the demands you face.

You need to seek some *variety* in your life, but not too much. The balance between the need for novelty, unpredictability and variety on the one hand and for routine and space to plan your life on the other depends to an extent on your personality. However, almost everyone has a tipping point beyond which change stops being exciting and instead becomes stressful and exhausting. While some aspects of the pattern of your life are beyond your control, do look for the choices you have and try to find a lifestyle that suits you. This may need some negoti- ation with your spouse, partner, friends or colleagues.

Seek *clarity*. Ambiguity is stressful and inefficient, but so often we soldier on at home or at work not really knowing what is expected of us because we don't want to seem stupid, demanding or pernickety. Ask the stupid question; it's remarkable how often an invaluable flash of insight results when you have the courage to do so. Having clear expectations from your spouse isn't unromantic, it's liberating, because then there aren't any hidden traps to fall into. You may remember me saying this before if you've read others of my books, but my wife is great at telling me what she needs. Occasionally, she'll say to me: 'Tim, it's been a while since you bought me flowers. I'd love it if you bought me some.' 'All right,' say I. The next day I go and buy a bunch of flowers and then come home and present them to my wife, whereupon she exclaims: 'They're beautiful, thank you. What a lovely surprise!' That's real clarity, and the result is pleasure all round. She gets flowers, and I get to feel I'm a good husband.

At work, all good managers give clear directives. If yours doesn't, ask for clarification whenever you need to. If this doesn't work, your boss, or maybe the whole organization, is toxic. You may need to consider your career options. Is it time to make a career move, do you need to change your way of working, or do you need to talk more to colleagues so as to build a better support network? I don't have all the answers for you, but I do know that working without aims and objectives can grind you down, so you need to do something rather than letting yourself become a victim of workplace toxicity.

Respect can be elusive. You really can't demand respect; it doesn't work that way. But you can choose to hang out with people who are respectful. You can seek involvement with organizations or groups that are respectful. For example, football supporters tend to respect other supporters of the same club; you're a member of a tribe. Many churches have members who are mutually supportive and respectful. There are many examples; my point is that you need to put yourself where you're likely to be valued. This can be difficult if you don't value yourself, but it's crucial. If you take nothing else from this book, please don't stay with someone who doesn't respect you. A very wise therapist friend of mine had only three questions of a client to determine whether or not her relationship had legs. They were: 'Do you like him? Do you respect each other? And can you be yourself with him?' If the answer to any of those was no, the client was advised that the future of the relationship was bleak. Whether there was love in the relationship was to my friend of secondary importance. That can come later. But without affection, respect and honesty, the relationship is dead in the water.

Reach out to good people for *support*. Particularly at times of need. Don't be embarrassed to display your needs; most people are pleased and flattered to be needed and to be asked to help. If you get a negative response when you ask for support, at least you've flushed out a false friend. Try to surround yourself with people who are as supportive of you as you are of others. You're not asking for special treatment, just to get something back in any friendship. This won't always happen because life isn't fair, but you have choice over who your friends are.

Since I brought it up, don't look for *fairness*, look for opportunity. Accept the bouquet which life gives you despite you not having earned it. Accept the unfairnesses, too. If they happen occasionally, that's life. If they happen constantly, you're being given a message. You need to change something. If you're feeling resentful, there's something you are doing wrong. Don't blame the object of your resentment; they're just being them. It's you who need to take action, to change things. That's down to nobody but you.

Life usually gives you plenty of reminders when things need to change. A man walking by a tall building is killed when a piano falls on his head. At the gates of heaven he asks God why he let this happen. 'I did warn you,' replies God. 'What do you mean?' asks the man. 'Well, first there was the grain of sand I blew into your eye on the beach when it was windy and you should have been wearing sunglasses; you ignored that. Then there was the piece of wood which nearly hit you when you walked under a ladder; you ignored that, too. Then I sent the car when you were crossing the road while checking your texts, which nearly hit you. When you ignored that one you left me with no choice.' Try to attend to the repeated messages life offers you.

Every now and then, particularly if you're feeling unhappy or stressed, check out what you're thinking. Are you making judgements about yourself, the past or the future? If you are, what sort of judgements are they? Are you making harsh value judgements against yourself? Then make sure you'd be happy to make the same sort of evaluation of your dearest friend. If you wouldn't because it would be cruel and unfair, then you're using a double standard and you need to challenge it. Are you extrapolating from a misfortune you've suffered to conclude that things will always be this way? Try to reframe what happened – it could have been so much worse, you dodged a bullet, it'll probably get better. Look for any progress you've made. I'm much more interested in direction of travel than in where you are now. If you're making any changes in the right direction, you'll get there in the end.

Are you comparing yourself unfavourably with others? First, it's invalid because everyone is different. If my only measure of success in golf is whether or not I can be as good as Tiger Woods, I'm always going to come up short, be frustrated and fail to enjoy the game. If my aim is to bring my handicap down a bit, I've got a reasonable chance of success and it'll be fun trying. Second, your judgement is almost certainly based on false premises. The mum at your son's school who always looks great, is involved with everything and has a spotless home probably has armies of helpers she doesn't tell you about, spends two hours in the morning on her make-up while her husband gets the kids ready for school, and is in fact on only one committee though she makes it sound like she's on dozens. Don't believe everything you see and hear.

Do a lot of your statements, particularly about yourself, contain the word 'should'? Try to reduce these value judgements and replace them with statements containing words such as 'choose', 'hope', 'like' and 'believe'.

I'll leave the issue of challenging your thinking there for now. This is one of the most important concepts in this book, which is why I'm returning to it several times and I'll do so once more in the section on cognitive therapy in Chapter 9.

Don't forget to 'act as if'. Even if you don't feel that way, try to act like a happy person. I don't mean that you should deny your sadness or fear, just that you should spend some of your time doing what you would do if you had hope and happiness.

Try to be altruistic. Do good things for others, as that's probably the most powerful way of getting happier. Be selective about who is the beneficiary of your charity, though. The person who demands the most from you probably shouldn't get anything other than a very firm boundary. You choose who gets the benefit of what you have to offer, not the person who shouts the loudest.

And finally, what is this *happiness* thing anyway and why are we trying to possess it all the time? The idea of happiness first appeared in literature over two millennia ago in the writings of the Greek philosopher Epicurus. He saw happiness as the absence of physical pain and mental anguish. He considered that this was best achieved through moderation in all things and the avoidance of extremes. In contrast, there is a trend in modern life to insist on constant happiness and to engage in a string of 'peak experiences' in order to achieve this. These experiences are all photographed, often using the dreaded selfie-stick, in order to provide proof that your life is one of uninterrupted happiness. The reality is, of course, very different; wonderful experiences are wonderful only because they are different. It is the contrasts in life which give it definition. If you really go from one amazing experience to another, all you'll feel is exhausted and the strain of keeping up the euphoric pretence will very likely make you miserable. Real connections with other people, which as I've stated are central to developing a positive and meaningful life, happen only when you stop for long enough to share genuine feelings and experiences. This won't happen through Facebook. Clinical depression is several times more common in Western cultures than in Eastern ones. The psychologist Brock Bastian (author of *The Other Side of Happiness: Embracing a More Fearless Approach to Living*) explains this with the observation that in Japan and China positive and negative experiences are both seen as essential and of equal value, with neither being sought or avoided, but both being accepted as valuable parts of life.

Acceptance of feelings, moods and events, good and bad, is the only route I know to contentment. You can be content to be sad right now, because that is the emotion which belongs in your life at this particular moment. So maybe what we're looking for isn't happiness at all but contentment achieved through acceptance of what is.

7

Coping with the toxic stuff

Apocryphally attributed to former British Prime Minister Harold Macmillan is the answer to the question of what he most feared in politics: 'Events, dear boy, events.' I don't care whether it's true or not. If he didn't say it, he should have. The public life of a politician hangs on a thread which can be severed in an instant by adverse events. But then the same is true of the health and happiness of any of us. It would be lovely if everything always proceeded the way we planned it, but few are fortunate enough to enjoy such an uncomplicated life. Most of us are subject from time to time to loss, adversity and people who mess up our lives. So a large part of staying happy and healthy is learning how to deal with these threats to our wellbeing.

Loss and grief

The most obvious type of loss is grief resulting from the death of someone you love, but here I'm talking about all forms of major loss and the grief they cause: loss of financial security, loss of a cherished hope, loss of self-esteem, loss of your job or your house and, yes, loss of the love of your life through separation, divorce or death. All loss leaves you bereft, feeling that your world is empty and of less value than it was before. After an initial period of numbness which may last minutes or months, many suffer a period of grief that is crippling, hopeless and black. The more you try to put on a brave face, the more it brings you crashing to the ground under its weight. So what is to be done?

The answer is to experience it rather than avoid it. That may seem obvious, but I've seen too many people whose problems stem from trying to escape their grief. Early in my career I saw a lady whose unhappiness had lasted 40 years. Throughout this time she had engaged in a very successful life, achieving everything she had wanted to, except for happiness. Through the course of therapy she discovered that the root of her sadness was a miscarriage which she had suffered in her early twenties. She had been told to forget about it, just to get on with her life and try for another pregnancy. There was no funeral, no acknowledgement of her loss and no space to grieve. The result was a slow-burning grief that extended through her life.

How long will your grief last? I don't know for certain, but I can say this: your loss will never be OK. Of course it won't. Whatever you value or whoever you love is dear to you for a reason. Grief is horrid, and life isn't ever the same again. But that doesn't mean that your life is over or that it is worthless. How you feel now doesn't last forever. What comes back is the texture in your life and the choice. The texture is between times when you feel sad and other times when you feel other things, even sometimes happiness. I know that sounds impossible, but it's true – *if* you let yourself feel what you feel rather than chasing your feelings away. The choice is about feeling sad when you choose to and not at inopportune moments when it hits you like a punch to the solar plexus. Life gets its shades of meaning back, the ups and downs, the light and the dark. This happens when it happens, but it does happen.

So be patient if you can. Turn to your friends and anyone who loves you and keep feeling. Whatever you do, don't tell yourself to 'get over it', 'pull yourself together' or 'toughen up'. That's not how it works, and you wouldn't say it to anyone else. If you would, then you need a book on how to be better at kindness, empathy and wisdom. But you wouldn't, I know that, so work on being kinder and more understanding of yourself. Don't expect much of yourself right now. You need time to lick your wounds, but don't withdraw completely; try to look after yourself. Even if it feels like going through the motions, keep taking some exercise, eat healthily, don't lose touch with your friends and do a bit of what you would enjoy if you could enjoy anything. Actions come first, feelings return later.

Other major life events and ongoing difficulties

It's not just loss and grief which can bring you down, but any major change, even welcome ones. We're not well designed to absorb major changes in our lives, so if you are going through an upheaval, treat yourself with kid gloves. That promotion at work, that move to a better office, that much anticipated holiday abroad, that house move, that unexpected windfall. It's all great, but it's all a shock to the system. Actuaries, who are paid to assess risk of getting ill, will tell you that all major changes increase your risk of illness. Being aware of this is half the battle. The other half is taking action to protect yourself.

Some events are more stressful than others. We've discussed bereavement, separation, divorce and other losses. Add to those developing a chronic or life-threatening illness or caring for someone else who has. Or battling to keep afloat when you are unemployed and in poverty. And then there is living in fear, for example waiting for results of medical tests or waiting to find out if your job is going to be lost in the next round of redundancies, or whether your mortgage company will foreclose on you before you find your next job. It's no surprise that these are times when you are at risk of stress-related illness. What is more surprising is that having small kids to look after puts you at risk. It does.

If you are facing life events or ongoing difficulties alone, you need to put keeping yourself in one piece at the top of your list of priorities. Your kids, your job, the person you care for or whatever are important, but most important of all right now is you. Spend some time on yourself, however busy you are. It's OK to ask for support, to sit your kids in front of the TV for a while so you can have a lie down, or do some of what you love or what you would love if you hadn't forgotten how to focus on yourself. You're going to need time to get good at relaxation, mindfulness and thought-challenging; learning those skills is going to take some time. Take it.

Imagine you were supporting a dear friend through the challenges you're facing. What would you advise her? Take your own advice. For the sorts of people who suffer from stress-related conditions, usually those who habitually focus on the needs of others rather than their own, acting like a loving friend to themselves tends to be very hard, but it is crucial. You can't be of any use to others if you are in pieces because of self-neglect. Look at someone you know who is able to look after themselves and copy them. I don't mean turning into a selfish and horrible person, but I do mean shifting the balance so that you don't just survive but thrive through the difficulties you face. That's simply wise husbandry of you as a resource.

People

As I pointed out in Chapter 1, the chances are that a person or people lie behind your stress-related problems, so you're going to need to learn how to deal with them. People tend to be the most enriching and the most toxic factors in our lives. Learning how to cope with toxic people is central to developing resilience.

First, get ready by identifying the good people in your life who you can turn to when you need to and be ready to reach out to them. It takes some doing to get in the habit of asking for support if you've never done it before, but it's very important. The old adage that 'a problem shared is a problem halved' is wrong – it's reduced by more than that. There is a host of research showing that support is highly protective against stress-related illness.

Next, recognize who in your life is toxic to you. I'll call him Jim, though she could just as easily be Jill. This isn't making a value judgement, as earlier I advised you to minimize those. You're not saying that Jim is a bad person; you're just recognizing that he isn't good for you. So do you feel uncomfortable whenever you're with him? Or tired? Or fearful? Or less good about yourself? Do you feel constantly pushed or obligated to do things for him? Do you do far more for him than he does for you? Do you feel that you don't have any choices when you're with him? Are you constantly waiting for him to present the next drama or crisis? Is he kind to you, or not really? If it weren't for the fact that he says he is your friend or that he's family, would you say he acts as a friend to you? Is the only reason you assume you couldn't cope without him that he tells you that's the case? If you have very firm boundaries and are super-assertive, Jim may be easily managed; but if you're one of life's givers, there may be a risk you'll be bled dry by him.

You see where I'm going with this. Ask yourself the right questions and it becomes fairly clear that Jim is toxic to you. So then what? The next step is asking yourself why you have him in your life. If the only answer is that you feel you should, you probably shouldn't. The same is true if you fear loneliness and believe that nobody else will fill the space if you don't have Jim at the centre of your life. Good people appear when there is space for them. If Jim is taking all of you, then nobody else will emerge, because kind, generous people tend to hang back and come only when invited.

The thing is that toxic people are often better at being toxic than you are at protecting yourself from them. They've been perfecting their skills at being the way they are all their lives. So while I would like to help you change the dynamics of your relationship so that it works better for you, in practice this may be difficult. Sometimes if your car keeps breaking down, it may be wiser to dump it and get a new one than to keep trying to fix it, accepting that it's broken and beyond repair. Sometimes relationships are like that. I'm not saying you should expel your best friend the first time you fall out or divorce your husband the first time you don't see eye to eye, but I am saying that if all the evidence points to Jim doing you more harm than good over a long period, you should seriously consider the future of your relationship.

If you fear Jim's reaction if you were to reject him, I can understand that. Presuming Jim is forceful, good at being hurtful, or is manipulative, you may rightly anticipate that he won't take your rejection lying down. If you lack confidence, the prospect of Jim's anger at being rebuffed may be scary. This is when you need to ask for support from the people who really care about you. This isn't disloyal, even though Jim may tell you it is. He would, wouldn't he? He wants to control you and you getting support from others threatens his ability to do so. Stand firm. Everyone is entitled to the support of friends and family. Don't let yourself be gaslighted if you can avoid it. If you don't know what gaslighting is, go and look it up. Do you recognize yourself in the description?

Right now, are you thinking you don't have any friends to turn to? Are you sure? What about the friendly person you know at work? What about your priest, your doctor, the lady you often chat to in the coffee shop at the railway station? Anybody you can talk to and trust, who won't use your confidence as fuel for salacious gossip or insist on you following their advice. Remember, *a friend is someone who is friendly, a mother someone who is motherly, a father someone who is fatherly* and so on. If there really is nobody, OK, I understand. Jim may have skilfully isolated you from your friends. You may be on your own. Then *be the best friend you can to yourself.* This means talking to yourself and treating yourself as you would a good and much loved friend. When Jim tells you what a useless person you are or says that your rejection has ruined his life, imagining that you are this friend and that you are commiserating, advising and encouraging the real you is what you need to do right now. It's easy when it's someone else saying: 'Stand up for yourself! He's just lashing out because he's sad and angry. Don't believe him – you're a good person, and you can do better than Jim.' That's what you'd say to your friend, or something like that, right? OK, so say it to yourself. You need your support right now, so make sure you give it to yourself.

I've assumed here that the relationship under discussion is beyond saving and that the person who is toxic to you isn't married to you or a first-degree relative. I'm not going to advise you to end your marriage or abandon your family. That has to be your decision taken after a lot of soul searching. But I can tell you what my limits would be. Physical violence, intimidation, regular humiliation or cruelty – those to me would spell the end of a relationship, even if the relationship was based on genetics or betrothal. You have to work out what your limits are. They may be different from mine, but be clear about this: if you accept abuse in any form without setting a limit with consequences attached, you are voting for the abuse to continue. If you accept the role of victim, you are choosing it.

So what limits can you set? A start is to state clearly that what was said or done to you is unacceptable. That may seem obvious, but I've seen a lot of victims of abuse who tolerate their abuse in silence. If speaking up is too dangerous, you really need to get out of the situation. Nobody should accept being bullied into silence – that's torture. If your abuser merely laughs in your face, you need to work out a consequence. This may range from 'If this happens again, I will leave the room', through 'If you insult me, you can make your own supper' to 'If you lay a finger on me again, I will leave you.' Whatever the consequence is, you must be prepared to carry it through. As often as not, though, all that is needed is for the person you feel abused by to know that's what you're experiencing for it to stop, as in: 'When you make fun of me in front of your friends I feel humiliated. Please stop it.' 'But I'm just joking, you shouldn't be so sensitive,' he replies. 'Whether I'm sensitive or not isn't the point. I'm asking you to stop it as it makes me unhappy.' Apart from a bit of harrumphing, shrugging of the shoulders and looking heavenwards, that is probably the end of the interaction. You've achieved a change in the dynamics of your relationship and voted for being treated with respect, which is a triumph. Don't expect a round of applause for this. Jim is used to getting his own way, and you getting tough is a shock. He won't like it when that changes, but in time he'll accept it.

Then there's gameplaying (see Chapter 1). Here the inter-action is more complex. You need to analyse the game, determine the payoff and then design an antithesis. To remind you, an antithesis is a manoeuvre designed to prevent the gameplayer from getting his payoff. Let's return to the game I described in Chapter 1, when I was irritable and looking for a row after a tough day at work. I manoeuvred my wife into an argument so I could unload my spleen on her. What antithesis would you choose? There are loads of them; just don't give me the payoff of an argument. 'Oh, I see, you're tired and irritable, I understand. I'm not going to argue with you, though' would be one. Stating that you understand the subtext, what is really going on, is often a powerful antithesis as the interaction is no longer covert, which it has to be for the payoff to work.

The key is that if you're in a relationship in which someone is routinely putting you in a position which you haven't chosen, by covert means, don't get angry, get thinking. Analyse the game, discover the payoff and then design an antithesis. As always, talking this through with a trusted friend will probably help.

If you need more help with this, read Eric Berne's book *Games People Play*, particularly the second half, which describes the games. It's a hoot. There's more on dealing with people in my book *Toxic People: Coping with Dysfunctional Relationships*.

If you keep meeting people who use and abuse you, this isn't coincidence. Users and abusers are very good at finding people they can take from. Just keep removing them from your life. That'll be scary, as they'll tell you that you're a loser who is only worth anything because of them. But draw yourself up to your full height and show them the door. And be prepared to do that over and over, until eventually someone will drift into your life who doesn't abuse you. Every fibre of your body will tell you to reject the people who are kind to you, but resist this urge. In fact, go looking for kind people; they are out there; they just don't come forward and press themselves on you like the takers do. You need to do some of the work in getting good people in your life, but it's worth it.

8

Kindness, consistency, persistence and pacing

I don't know about you, but for me the most important quality a person can have is kindness. I can forgive all sorts of shortcomings in someone if they are kind. In fact, in my view kindness is greatly undervalued in our society. Beauty, strength, athleticism, success, wealth, wit, toughness – all these attributes are valued. Just look at a newspaper or a glossy magazine and you'll see celebrities or leaders being admired for having these qualities, but kindness? Not so much; it's boring. At business school, do they teach you how to be kind to employees? Like heck they do. Are we modern citizens, proud as we are of our civilized values, always full of the milk of human kindness? That'll be a 'no'. And it makes no sense, because kindness works. It's efficient. There are lots of research studies showing that simple acts of kindness are immensely healing to those suffering from stress-related illnesses and just as many showing that kindness in management is more productive than ruthlessness or punitiveness. The press doesn't often report acts of kindness, and this quality is sometimes even less evident in its reporting. Many of us tend to focus on a few narrow aspects of our beliefs which fit our own agenda, while ignoring the oft-repeated instructions of our spiritual leaders to show love to one other. Is that a bit harsh? Maybe, but I hope you take my point: loving kindness is what makes the world go round.

Forgiveness is the most difficult form of kindness to pull off, but incredibly healing if you can manage it. The best example I know of is the Truth and Reconciliation Commission in South

Africa. When Nelson Mandela's ANC took over power from the white minority government they could have gone on a rampage of revenge against the people who had persecuted them. They didn't, instead inviting those who had done bad things when in power to confess their guilt, whereupon the miscreants were forgiven, even those who had done some truly awful things. Hence the inter-racial wounds began to heal. That was for me goodness and wisdom which shines a light through time. It required admission of guilt though. What if there is no such admission? What if the person who has harmed you or a loved one has never admitted their wrongdoing? That for me is the greatest challenge life can give you. I know what I'd like to be able to do, which is to forgive everybody, but it's really hard. Those familiar with the Bible will know that Christ was able to forgive the people who had him nailed to a tree. Not many could manage that, but I have met some people who have managed forgiveness after dreadful things have been done to them and I have seen how their success in forgiving has been a weight off their shoulders.

A few years ago a white supremacist entered a church in my home town of Charleston, South Carolina, which was attended by a mostly African American congregation, shooting several of them dead for no other reason than their race. More than one family member of the deceased expressed forgiveness of the killer. The amazing grace of these words brought the community, white and black, together in a way that was wonderful to behold.

I can't give you an algorithm for achieving forgiveness, though if you're religious, prayer may help, and as I'll explain in the next chapter, mindfulness can, too. Do try for it, because it is very healing.

Given how effective kindness is when bestowed on others, it's not surprising that kindness to yourself is a cornerstone of resilience. But it's so difficult to practise as it flies in the face of everything we have been taught. If someone tells you that you are full of 'self-love', they aren't complimenting you. Surely, though, there's nothing wrong with treating yourself as a loved one, so long as you love others, too. I don't mean loving yourself to the exclusion of others, but treating yourself lovingly so that you have more strength to give love to others. This is one of those many areas requiring balance: balance between caring for yourself and caring for others. Ignore the former and you've got nothing to give of the latter.

Maybe you spend all your time looking after the needs of one or more other people because you fear their disapproval. But if the only way of getting a person's approval is by acting as their servant, maybe their approval isn't worth having. Putting it another way, the only way of finding out whether someone really cares about you is by stopping giving everything to him and instead seeking a balanced give-and-take relationship.

But it's you that I'm most concerned about. Others may hurt you, but the person who gives you the most hurt is you. That needs to stop. Bullying is wrong even if the only person you bully is yourself. Criticizing yourself every time you make a mistake or come up short is bullying. I'm not advocating special treatment for you here, just *consistency*. By this I mainly mean consistency between how you treat yourself compared with how you treat others. But I also mean how you treat yourself at different times or in different situations. It's easy to give yourself a pat on the back when you succeed or achieve something. Much more telling is whether you treat yourself with compassion and respect when you make a mistake. In this context, try to minimize the amount of rough self-talk you engage in. 'Oh, you stupid idiot, how could you mess that up?' might seem like a harmless admonition, but would you speak to someone else like that? No? Too disrespectful, too cruel? Then it won't do for you, either. Remember, *punishment doesn't work* and harsh self-talk is punishing. Now, if you've been deliberately cruel, careless, selfish, greedy or lazy, a modicum of self-criticism is appropriate, but it has to be proportionate to the lapse, not excessive and not of a degree which will injure your confidence or self-esteem. The purpose of critical reflection is to learn, so as to avoid future lapses of the same kind. You won't learn anything if you beat yourself up. Even self-criticism must be delivered kindly. And remember that *life isn't a game of perfect.* Try for mostly good, not perfect; perfect isn't sustainable.

This charitable disposition towards yourself is one key to achieving *persistence.* You can keep going if you don't feel beaten down and humiliated by your shortcomings. Whatever field of endeavour I'm engaged in, I would prefer to have at my side someone who has made mistakes, acknowledged them and learned from them than someone supremely talented who has breezed through every previous challenge without breaking into a sweat. In my experience, persistent graft wins out against pretty showboating in the end. You achieve the ability to graft through difficulties and reverses by avoiding the emotional scars which come from excessive self-criticism.

The other key to persistence is honesty. When you don't achieve your objective or you feel humiliated, don't pretend you don't care, particularly to yourself. I know why you do it; it's to protect yourself and your feelings. But denial that your endeavour mattered leads to becoming detached. You lose sight of the fact that it was worthwhile. If it didn't matter, you might as well give up. So there's another project abandoned, another opportunity missed. Instead, recognize the reverse for what it was: a temporary setback. By all means be disappointed, but realize that if you keep going, treating yourself kindly and respectfully along the way, you'll get there in the end. Of course, this presumes your aims were realistic in the first place. If you've begun to doubt that, turn to a friend you trust and check with her whether what you were attempting was reasonable and achievable.

Apologies to those of you who are bored by sport, but I do think that some of these principles show up very clearly in top-class sporting contests. I'll come back with more examples later on, but I'll give one now. I was watching a cricket Test match at Lord's between England and Australia with a friend who was not a regular watcher of the game. This was 20 years or so ago, when Australia were on their way to becoming the dominant team in world cricket. On this day they were batting and were handing England the customary drubbing. My friend made a comment about the England fielders which gave me pause for thought: 'They don't seem to be trying,' she said. 'Look, that man isn't even running after the ball like he cared.' She was right. The England team were ambling around as if playing a family game on the beach. Why? Because they knew Australia were the better team and likely to win. Rather than try their guts out and be humiliated by their inferiority, they protected their egos by pretending to themselves that the result didn't matter. They lost the series by a 5–0 whitewash, if my memory serves me correctly. Contrast this with the attitude of the same Australian team when they lost a series in India shortly afterwards. Their captain was asked for his reflections after their defeat. He wasn't downcast, but admitted that his team had lost to the better team in those conditions. 'I'll tell you what though, mate,' he concluded, 'we'll learn from this and come back stronger.' They did, and were soon recognized as one of the best teams ever to have played the game. Learning and getting stronger through cheerful recognition of your shortcomings: the surest way to get better and stronger.

And so to the importance of pacing yourself. In my experience most people who suffer from stress-related illness comprise the good, honest givers of the world, the best among us. They give so much because they feel they should. Lacking a solid self-esteem, they seek to disprove their own hypothesis of worthlessness by giving so much to others that they hope they will gain their approval. The trouble is that, as already established, this leads to them becoming surrounded by takers. Beyond this, it inevitably leads to disillusionment and exhaustion. You can't give anything your all, all the time; that's not the way we're designed. And impressing people is pointless. It may make you feel less bad about yourself for a while, but the benefit doesn't last. Not even if the person impressed is your boss. Do as good a job as you sustainably can, and the rewards and recognition will eventually follow – not immediately when they are deserved but, with persistence, eventually. The only person's approval you really need, though, is yours. If you can recognize that your efforts are worthwhile even if they aren't bearing fruit yet and even if they aren't recognized by anyone else, you'll get somewhere worthwhile in the end. Not maybe your intended destination, but worthwhile nonetheless. If you want to achieve as much as you possibly can, pace yourself. The runner who completes the first mile of a marathon in four minutes won't win the race. Life is a marathon, not a sprint.

OK, I'm going to preen my feathers a little now. I think you'll forgive me for that (maybe try it yourself occasionally). As an eight-year-old boy I was mad keen on cricket. I wanted to be Ken Barrington (the best batsman of the age and a lovely, self-effacing man). I signed up for all the coaching I could get and practised my little heart out. I never made it into the school first XI, not in junior school anyway. Many years later, as an adult, I happened to be looking through my late father's papers and came upon my school report from that age written by the head of sports. It read: 'Tim is the most dedicated student of the game I have ever met. Unfortunately, he is lamentably lacking in talent.' Written over the report in my father's writing were the words: 'Do not show Tim.' He was kind, my dad. But I didn't give up. I struggled through the various levels of school cricket with limited success, which, having a realistic appreciation of my limitations, I accepted easily enough. I eventually found a bowling technique which allowed me to generate a lot of swing (curve balls if you're American). It allowed me a surprising amount of success for some years, and in the end I became captain of my university cricket team. The point of this story is that talent only goes so far. If you stick at stuff, you can usually succeed. So long as you don't get in your own way, by trying too hard too soon or beating yourself down. Slow and steady, ease your way forward. Take the hits and accept the reverses. Learn from your mistakes and keep going, particularly when things aren't going your way.

So I've laboured this point enough. Rethink your life strategy. Look after yourself. You'll achieve more if you do, regardless of how low your estimate of your value.

I don't know if you've ever read any of Bill Bryson's books. He's one of my favourite authors because of his keen observations and even sharper wit, which makes me laugh a lot. He's my opposite in that he is an American who emigrated to the UK and he has a lot to say about his adopted country. One of his pet peeves is shops in pretty English villages which exclusively stock items like tea towels, mugs and little pieces of wood with inspirational messages on them. He sees these as an irritating waste of time. This is one of the few subjects on which I disagree with him. Choose the right messages and look at them regularly, particularly when you're in a funk. Try 'Life is a marathon, not a sprint', 'Good is better than perfect', 'Be to yourself as you are to others', or whatever else is the reminder you need.

9

Techniques and treatments

If you're really struggling with severe depression, anxiety or any other stress-related condition, please visit your GP, be honest about what you're experiencing and ask to be referred for therapy. It works. In this chapter I will outline some of the available treatments and some helpful skills. Even if you don't need formal treatment, what I'm going to describe may be of help in enabling you to change the way you think and act. Change may be what you need right now. If your life has been heading nowhere, turn around and head somewhere else. Having said that, don't expect instant results from any of what follows. You'll need to keep going with it, but if you do, these techniques and treatments can improve your life enormously.

Relaxation

Relaxation exercises can be immensely powerful in developing resilience if you persevere with them, enabling you to reduce your level of arousal in challenging environments to a level at which you can function at your best. A cool head is crucial in the heat of battle, and expertise in relaxation can give you that regardless of what you're facing. The following exercise has appeared in a number of my earlier books, so you may already be familiar with it. There are many variations on this theme, and the thing is to find the one which works best for you. There are several relaxation exercises available as apps, audio files or other spoken word media. Look on Amazon or on Apple's App Store if that's what suits you best. Some people benefit from yoga techniques or transcendental meditation learned in a group setting. Others find following a set of written instructions more helpful, allowing them to do the exercise at their own pace with their own mental imagery. What follows is just one example of such a technique, but one which many of my patients have found helpful.

Whichever way you choose to learn the technique, it needs a lot of practice. Here's the thing: relaxation exercises are a total waste of time *to begin with*. In fact, they may make you feel worse initially, because they don't work straight away, which may be dispiriting. Doing anything and feeling like you're failing at it tends to get you down, though I hope less so by the time you finish this book.

But please do persevere, because when you master the exercise you will find that it changes your life. You're doing it not for benefit now but as an investment in the future. The people who benefit the most from relaxation exercises are those who put them at the top of their list of priorities and practise for half an hour every day, no matter how busy or stressed they are. If you hear that an asteroid is going to vaporize your town in 24 hours, by all means run for the hills, but only after you've done your relaxation practice for the day.

Looking back, I did this relaxation exercise daily for about three years when I was at medical school and early in my medical career, not because I suffered extraordinary levels of anxiety but because I realized I needed a way of getting through the very challenging final medical exams and house jobs (the first year of medical practice, which many find terrifying). It took me about a month of daily practice to find the exercise of any use at all, and then only when I was feeling quite calm anyway. It was at least three months before I was able to use it when I was under strain, such as before an exam, because the hardest time to perform a relaxation exercise effectively is when you actually need it, when you're under high levels of stress. In about two to three years I reached the point I'm at now, where I no longer need to do the full exercise because I can switch on a relaxed state like a light when I need it. I think I'm a bit slow, as I'm told that the average time to achieve this level of expertise is about nine months, but who cares? I got there in the end and it changed my life. I can tell you from personal experience that the time and effort it takes to become proficient at a relaxation exercise are worth it.

A relaxation exercise

Spend 20–30 minutes on this exercise.

1 Find a suitable place to relax. A bed or easy chair is ideal, but anywhere will do, preferably somewhere quiet and private. Once you are good enough at the exercise to find it useful, do it when you need it. Until then, do it when you've got time and are calm enough to be able to concentrate on it.
2 Try to clear your mind of thoughts as far as you can.
3 Take three very slow, very deep breaths (allow 10–15 seconds to breathe in and out once).
4 Imagine a neutral image. An example may be the number 1. Don't choose any object or image with emotional significance, such as a ring, a person or a banknote. Let the image fill your mind. See it in your mind's eye, give it a colour and a texture, try to see it in 3D; if it's a word, repeat it to yourself under your breath many times over. Continue until it fills your mind.
5 Slowly change to imagine yourself in a quiet, peaceful and pleasant situation. This might be a favourite place, an imagined situation or a happy scene from your past. Be there and notice all the feelings in each sense: see it, feel it, hear it, smell it, taste it. Spend some time there.

6   Slowly change focus to become aware of your body. Notice any tension in any part of your body. Take each group of muscles in turn and tense them, then relax them two or three times each. Include your fingers, hands, wrists, arms, shoulders, neck, face, chest, tummy, buttocks, thighs, legs, ankles, feet and toes. Be aware of the feeling of relaxation in contrast to how tense these muscles felt. When the process is complete, spend some time in this relaxed state. If you aren't relaxed, don't worry; you're just practising for now.

7   If you're doing the exercise during the day, slowly get up and go about your business. If it's bedtime, just lie in bed until you drop off to sleep (this is when you're practised at it; remember that to begin with it may not work).

At step 5, I need to emphasize that this isn't just visualization. It is a multi-sensory experience. Let me illustrate the point. You're imagining yourself on a beautiful Caribbean beach. Lovely, but not enough. Which direction is the wind coming from? Is it a steady breeze, or gusty? What does the sun feel like on your skin and does the temperature change when the sun goes behind a cloud? How would you describe the smell of hot sun on sand and of your suntan lotion? Is the sand soft or hard, smooth or lumpy? Describe the taste of your drink. How far back from where you're sitting does the grass start? Are the palm trees small, ornamental palms, or tall coconut palms? Are the coconuts green or brown? What can you hear? Are the waves crashing or lapping? Can you hear any seagulls or other sounds?

So you need to be there in every sense. This takes quite a lot of practice to pull off for most people.

Don't hurry this exercise and remember to practise every day. It will work eventually and when it does you'll be a lot more resilient.

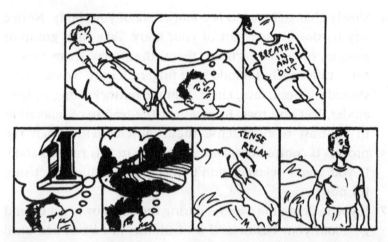

Figure 9.1

Time management

Many of my patients suffering from stress-related conditions spent most of their time rushing around in ever-decreasing circles. Life is busy, particularly if you have a demanding job, young children, a needy family or a lack of support. But on the whole it wasn't that which fuelled my patients' stress. It was either that they were trying to do the undoable or were trying to do everything at once.

In this context be aware of the 3 × multiplier – that is, the task you plan to complete will usually take around three times as long as you think. Since my retirement I've had the time and spare attention to observe this principle in action in my wife, who is always on the go. It holds true most of the time. So if you think you can do the shopping, clean the house, go over to help your mother with her laundry, work on your tax return and prepare supper, I've got news for you: you can't. So make a rough estimate of how long you think each task will take, multiply by three and then be realistic in only trying to fit in what can be done in the time available. Prioritize, and remember to plan in some down time, too. The human body isn't designed for perpetual motion.

Yes, I know, if you're a single mother without a support system there's little opportunity to rest. But if any arises, take it. Sitting the kids in front of the TV for long enough for you to take a rest is in their interests as well as yours. If you do have friends or family offering support, use them. And if you're married, what's the point in a husband anyway, unless you get him to do stuff?

But it's not just the weight of demands on your time which is the problem, it's also how you organize it. If you're overwhelmed, stop, take the 30 minutes which you don't have and make a time plan. This means organizing tasks together in the most efficient way possible. This can be done on the spot covering the rest of today, or in advance, covering the few days or week ahead. The time plan shown in Figure 9.2 is a weekly one for a single business executive without children. Yours will probably look very different, but it's the principle that matters. Organizing your time so that you're doing things together which can be done in one place and building in spaces and breaks for unforeseen circumstances will make your life run a lot more smoothly and reduce your stress levels significantly.

	Monday	Tuesday	Wednesday	Thursday	Friday	Saturday	Sunday
9 am				filing	deliver report	shopping	↑
10 am	admin meeting	spare for crisis and problems	personal work	computer work	travel		
11 am				prepare report	meet with client		
12 am							
1 pm		L	U N	C H			rest
2 pm	personal work	travel meeting	presentation	meeting about report	travel personal work	rest	
3 pm			rest				
4 pm			travel	admin	prepare next week's time plan		
5 pm							
Evening	rest	prepare presentation	late meeting	going out	rest	theatre	↓

Figure 9.2 Time plan

I came upon this principle fairly late in my career, but goodness me, how it helped: running clinics near each other rather than crisscrossing the county; building in admin time; letting patients know that I'd return their calls at the end of the day (except emergencies) ... Best of all was advertising appointments as of 40 minutes' duration while placing them 45 minutes apart – time to deal with the unforeseen without running late and having to deal with disgruntled patients who had been sitting and fuming in the waiting room. Planning my days better halved the stress of my job. Think about it.

Problem solving

This is the other organizational skill which you need to start getting good at. If you're buried under an enormous problem and feel crushed by the weight of it, don't flail about trying to solve it in one go. Divide and organize.

The thing with problems is that they don't come one at a time when you're ready for them, but at the most inopportune moments and, like London buses, several at a time. Some are conflicting, so solving one exacerbates another. The whole thing seems like a tangled mess, which leads to your brain becoming scrambled, logical thought flying out of the window, and either bad decisions being made or no decision at all, with denial or despair taking over. People who are overwhelmed tend to be irritable, particularly with those closest to them, which results in withdrawal of support just when you most need it.

The principle of problem solving is simple. Take a big problem or set of problems and split it/them up into smaller, manageable pieces. You may have seen the following example in one of my earlier books – I think it's a good one to illustrate the principle. You're in a financial mess. The problem is enormous and unmanageable. So split it up:

1 I'm above my overdraft limit at the bank.
2 My creditors are beginning to issue threats.
3 My outgoings exceed my income.
4 I have a lot of debtors who show no sign of paying what they owe me.
5 The interest rate is rising, meaning my monthly mortgage payments are increasing.
6 My car is getting old and increasingly expensive to run.
7 Christmas is a month away and I can't afford presents for the kids.

So now, rather than one gigantic mess, you have a defined set of problems to consider. They are linked, but nonetheless take each one separately. For each problem, brainstorm some actions which you could take. Include all your ideas, the good, the less good and the apparently downright silly (it's remarkable how often silly ideas turn out to be flashes of genius). So for problem 1 in the list above, possible actions might be:

- Arrange a meeting with my bank manager to request an increase in my overdraft limit.
- Explain that the problem is of cash flow and that I'm in the process of solving it. Point out that the same thing happened two years ago and I was back in the black within three months.
- Take out a short-term loan.
- Borrow from friends/relatives.
- Cut out items of expenditure (refer to separate expenditure list).
- Ignore it and hope it'll go away.
- Try to get more overtime at work.
- Sell the house and downsize.
- Look for a job with a better salary.
- Play the lottery.

Now think through each option in turn and rule out those which won't or are unlikely to work. Maybe talk them through with someone you trust.

Go through this process for each of the problems 1–7. You'll then come up with a list of action points, some of which will be listed more than once. Gather this list together and number in order of priority. Act on them one at a time, ticking each one off as you action it. Be realistic in the tasks you set yourself. Don't try to do everything in a day. The process needs to be sustainable and empowering, not exhausting and oppressive. Now you're doing everything you can to resolve your problems, which can liberate you from the tangle of confusion and despair you've been trapped in.

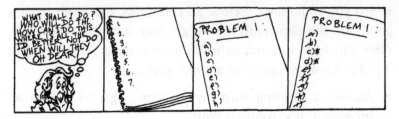

Figure 9.3

Of course, following this structure doesn't make your problems disappear overnight, but it does give you back some control and helps to reduce the fear which has been so paralysing.

Cognitive behavioural therapy (CBT)

The principles of CBT are so crucial to resilience and contentment that I've brought them up several times already, but in this section I'll look at how CBT works in a bit more detail.

I've often heard it said that the key to success and resilience under pressure is positive thinking. I disagree. What's the point in telling yourself that you're going to succeed when you haven't prepared and are facing a task or opponent above your level of ability? That way lies disillusionment. Do you want to put your boxing skills up against the heavyweight world champion? Best get a good reconstructive surgeon first. No, what you need is realistic thinking, together with a degree of acceptance (I'll come to that in the section on mindfulness below). Hubris is of use to no one, but neither is a distorted view of yourself, the world and the future in which you rate yourself and everything you touch negatively. That way lies avoidance and stagnation.

CBT is about identifying the thoughts which make up your negative cognitive triad (see Chapter 1) and then the deeply held underlying assumptions which generate these thoughts. Next, with the help of your therapist, you need to challenge these thoughts in a structured and logical way, setting up behavioural experiments to test each of the different ways of seeing the situation you face. Lastly, you compare, again with the help of your therapist, the results of these experiments with your pre-held thoughts and assumptions and decide how the evidence you have gathered may change them. This is an ongoing process, as our negative thoughts and assumptions have developed over a lifetime and so are tenacious. Just when you think you've got your thinking under control, a new set of negative and destructive thoughts pops up out of nowhere, reflecting a set of underlying assumptions of which you were previously unaware. You may be unaware that you assume you are uninteresting until your friend asks you to be his best man and you face having to give a speech. Each time an assumption like this is revealed you deal with it in the same structured way. This process is like dealing with a leaky boat. You deal with one leak only for another to appear, then another. Seal each leak and eventually the boat is seaworthy. It's about persistence. This is the 'cognitive' bit of CBT.

The 'behavioural' part of CBT involves getting good at relaxation, 'avoiding avoidance' (see Chapters 5 and 6) and other strategies I've outlined which you find helpful. This is based on the principles of *reciprocal inhibition* (you can't be anxious and relaxed at the same time) and *systematic desensitization* (working through your fears methodically in small steps) which I outlined in Chapter 6. It also reflects the principle that *you become the way you act*, so to change the way you think you have to change your behaviour first.

Let's look at an example of how CBT may work in practice. Say Danny is withdrawn and lonely because he thinks that any attempt to make friends or find a girlfriend will fail and humiliate him. His therapist starts by exploring these thoughts further. She finds that Danny has a set of assumptions which generate his negative thoughts and his withdrawal:

1 I'm ugly.
2 I'm boring.
3 I'm stupid.
4 People are cruel and critical.
5 If I get rejected, it's a disaster.
6 I will always be rejected.
7 Other people don't get rejected.

Next, Danny's therapist will ask him to rate his confidence in each of these assumptions, in percentage terms (how certain he is that the assumption is correct):

• I'm ugly: 100 per cent.
• I'm boring: 95 per cent.
• I'm stupid: 90 per cent.
• People are cruel and critical: 90 per cent.
• If I get rejected, it's a disaster: 80 per cent.
• I will always be rejected: 90 per cent.
• Other people don't get rejected: 80 per cent.

Some of these assumptions can be worked on straight away. For example, 'People are cruel and critical.' Danny has already told his therapist of an incident when he was being bullied at school. A boy he didn't know well had stepped in to challenge the bullies and stopped the incident in its tracks. The bullies were cruel, but what about the boy who helped him? If he wasn't cruel, is it possible that there are other generous people out there? Is it possible to find them? Now we're in much more productive territory. Then there's 'I'm boring'. How do you know? Do you find the same people interesting as your brother does? No? Why? Because you have different interests, different likes and dislikes? Oh, so it's not that you're boring to everyone then, but just those who aren't like you and don't share your interests. The same types of challenges can be made to each of these assumptions. Beauty is in the eye of the beholder. Achieving five GCSE passes probably puts you above average in terms of intelligence. Any sentence with 'always' in it is generally wrong (I was taught that by a tutor who showed me how to answer true/false exam questions to which I didn't know the answer). You get the picture. There's a lot of cognitive challenging that can happen in the therapy sessions.

But others of these assumptions will prove more tenacious. This is when behavioural experiments may be needed – for example, for assumptions 5–7, relating to rejection. These may not respond just to being challenged with discussion in the sessions; they may need to be tested out in real life. Danny's therapist doesn't ask him to try asking a girl out on a date, not yet. The very idea makes Danny panic, so she encourages him to start by trying something which he finds only slightly scary: asking a friendly male classmate, John, to meet him for coffee at a local coffee shop on Saturday to discuss a project their teacher has set for them. At their meeting, after the work part of the discussion is done, Danny tells John he is scared to ask a girl out on a date. John agrees that dating is scary and tells Danny about how a girl he liked at his last school had turned him down. John suggests asking Sally, who is on their project team, to join them to work on it next weekend. Danny does so the next day, but Sally says she's got a sporting event she's going to on Saturday, so she can't make it.

At the next session, Danny recounts all of this to his therapist, who praises him for what he's achieved. The fact that Sally didn't accept Danny's invitation to join him and John is irrelevant; he asked, which is a triumph. Now, after some processing of what happened, Danny is asked to re-rate the probabilities of points 5–7:

- If I get rejected it's a disaster: 50 per cent. (It depends on the context. On this occasion there was a reason for Sally not to come, so it wasn't too humiliating.)
- I will always be rejected: 20 per cent. (I still think that if it's just me, nobody will want to spend time with me, but I accept that John did, even if it was only to get the project done.)
- Other people don't get rejected: 10 per cent. (OK, I need to rephrase that because John told me about when he got rejected; other people don't get rejected as often as I do.)

So, as you can see, Danny and his therapist still have work to do, but already his assumptions are becoming less entrenched. More challenging and further behavioural experiments will take place over the following weeks, each one slowly working up to slightly more demanding encounters. When things don't go well, that's just grist to the mill of therapy. Life doesn't always cooperate with your best-laid plans, but engaging in this process will allow Danny to change, to think more realistically and to act more productively.

This is just a simple example to illustrate what may happen in CBT. It's a highly effective treatment for a host of psychological disorders and can help people who have no diagnosis at all, but are in a rut. The principles of CBT are a way of life which I recommend to everyone. I never let myself feel anxious, upset, angry or uncomfortable without CBTing myself. What am I thinking? Does it make sense? Is there a more realistic and helpful way of looking at my situation? Does that make me feel better? The answer is usually 'yes'.

If CBT is suggested, go for it. You may be amazed by the results. There are several different varieties of CBT, so don't worry if what you're offered doesn't exactly fit the model I've outlined. For example, one variant is called cognitive analytical therapy (CAT). This, as the name suggests, combines CBT with some exploration of the experiences and emotions from earlier in your life which brought you to where you are now. It suits some people, particularly those whose vulnerabilities have clear origins in early life trauma.

If you can't get a referral for CBT any time soon, try reading *The Feeling Good Handbook* by David Burns or visiting the website moodgym.com.au.

Mindfulness (mindfulness-based CBT – MBCBT)

Mindfulness as a treatment is an offshoot of CBT, and like CBT it's a way of life. Its principles are old, being based on Buddhist and other Eastern philosophies. It was introduced to a wider Western audience by Jon Kabat-Zinn, among others. He is the author of *Wherever You Go, There You Are: Mindfulness Meditation for Everyday Life*, which I highly recommend. He in turn followed the work of Eckhart Tolle, author of the bestseller *The Power of Now*, first published in 1997.

Tolle is an interesting character. If you want a longer description of how he discovered the principles which he writes about, you'll find it in my book *Overcoming Anxiety*. Better still, read *The Power of Now*. For our purposes, suffice it to say that Tolle learned through painful experience that it is impossible to be happy unless you spend most of your time in the present. Further, he would contend that it is quite difficult to be unhappy if you are present, unless you are suffering from chronic illness or pain. Most human suffering in communities not burdened by poverty comes from worrying about the past or the future. It's not the adversity you face which is the main cause of your misery, but you beating yourself up for allowing it to happen, railing against the injustice of it all, or fearing where it might all lead in the future. It's all a myth in any case; we all have selective memories and those who tend to depression or anxiety in particular tend to remember only what they got wrong, not what they could be proud of. And the stuff we worry about rarely happens. Most misfortune tends to fall without warning out of a clear blue sky. Your self-criticism and worries are fantasies from which you need to escape. You can do so by being truly present.

One of the best books on mindfulness is *Mindfulness: A Practical Guide to Finding Peace in a Frantic World* by Mark Williams and Danny Penman. The app *Headspace*, available for Apple and Android devices and (at the time of writing) free for the first ten days, is good for those who do best with something they can listen to. It has three basic guided meditations and then a library of topics to choose from, including stress, anxiety, cravings and others. The meditations last from three minutes to over 20 minutes, so as you become more expert, depending on how much time you have, you can increase the time you meditate. I'm told that the app *Calm* is also very good, though I haven't used it myself.

I may be accused of oversimplification, but for me mindfulness has just two main principles. The first, which I've touched on already, is being really *present* in the moment. I told you of my mindfulness test in Chapter 1 (being aware of the colour of the flowers outside my office). In your case, are you really aware of your surroundings and the experience they offer you right now?

If not, just take a moment to take them in and experience them before moving on to the next paragraph.

The second principle is to *stop fighting*. That means stop fighting with the past, the future, unfairness, your symptoms, your feelings and emotions, your failings and imperfections, everything. Just experience being. I like the injunction 'Don't just do something; sit there'. Living life fully requires you to be still for long enough to experience it. Many of my patients rush around at a million miles an hour in perpetual motion so as not to feel or experience pain and anguish. The trouble is that they then can't experience any joy either. A mindfulness therapist will encourage you to experience your emotions rather than running away from them. Uncomfortable feelings have a way of pushing through, however hard you try to push them away. Better to accept and even embrace them. That way they lose their power, like a ghost that you greet with a smile and a welcome. The spectre rattling his chains in the dead of night fails to be scary if you offer to polish his manacles.

Mindfulness, while being simple in principle, is tricky to pull off, so you may need some help with it. You may seek out an individual mindfulness therapist or a mindfulness group (it does seem to work well in a group setting and doesn't require much interaction, so should be manageable even if you're socially anxious). In any case, talk to your GP about it to see what may be available under the NHS.

Mindfulness is a powerful tool. A recent study of Buddhist monks showed that their brains are permanently changed by their practice of mindfulness-type meditation, allowing brain wave patterns most of us develop for only a few seconds at a time to persist for minutes to hours. These are the patterns which occur when you have a flash of inspiration, a moment of clarity or a sense of perfect peace. The most powerful form of meditation in producing this change, according to this research, involves forgiveness, which is no surprise given what we discussed in the previous chapter. Those learning it are encouraged to start by having forgiving thoughts towards people whom they love, but who have done something irritating or upsetting. They then move on to forgiving themselves for their own shortcomings and finish by meditating on forgiveness towards those whom they find most difficult or obnoxious. It's very challenging – give it a try. Mindful people are more robust, more creative, more productive and more often content than the rest of us. Their HPA axis (see Chapter 1) is recalibrated downwards, meaning that it takes much more to get them suffering from the effects of stress.

Just as mindfulness arose out of CBT, *acceptance and commitment therapy* (ACT) arose out of mindfulness. The focus is there in the name. Accept your situation, your symptoms and, even more, your limitations and difficulties. Don't try to escape them; let your feelings be. And let yourself be the way you are, rather than how you feel you should be. Observe your weaknesses rather than judging yourself for them, and – even harder for many – acknowledge your strengths. Forget the 'why' and work with what you have.

ACT could be a different acronym:

- Accept your reactions and stay present.
- Choose a valued direction.
- Take action.

While your feelings are what they are, you can control how you react to them. A therapist working with this model will agree with you a changed course of action and will encourage you to commit to it, however this makes you feel. This can be tough, because feelings are tough, particularly when they're caused by another person. 'Sticks and stones may break my bones, but ...' – I'm changing the proverb here – '... words hurt a lot worse.' That's why you may need a therapist to help you with difficult feelings while staying on your chosen course. Like the other therapies listed here, ACT is powerful and has a strong evidence base. If you want to read more about it try *Get Out of Your Mind & into Your Life: The New Acceptance and Commitment Therapy* by Steven Hayes and Spencer Smith.

There is a host of other psychological treatments which can help you to cope better with what life throws at you (exploratory psychotherapy and supportive counselling being two), but those outlined above are the ones I think it's worth everyone looking into. They have in common that they are a way of life. Maybe they represent a happier and more effective way of leading your life than the way you are leading it now?

10

Failing well

Theodore Roosevelt put it in a nutshell:

> It's not the critic who counts; not the man who points out
> how the strong man stumbles, or where the doer of deeds
> could have done them better. The credit belongs to the man
> who is actually in the arena, whose face is marred by dust
> and sweat and blood, who strives valiantly; who errs and
> comes up short again and again; because there is not effort
> without error and shortcomings; but who does actually
> strive to do the deed; who knows the great enthusiasm,
> the great devotion, who spends himself in a worthy cause,
> who at the best knows in the end the triumph of high
> achievement and who at the worst, if he fails, at least he fails
> while daring greatly.

I could end the book right there, so well did Teddy Roosevelt
sum up the wonderful power of failure over a hundred years
ago. This quote was brought to my attention by Dr Brené Brown
in a lecture entitled 'The Call to Courage', which you can find
on Netflix or on YouTube. It's well worth watching, and her
book *Daring Greatly* is equally worth reading.

Expanding on this quote, Dr Brown points out that winning
is sometimes showing up and losing, rather than running away,
and that in order to innovate, you have to be prepared to fail.
She sees courage and vulnerability not as opposites but as two
sides of the same coin. The courageous person allows herself to
be vulnerable rather than retreating to safety. She doesn't have
to look tough, because that's only the point if your aim in life is
to be admired by people shallow enough to believe your facade.

Courage is seeking something real, durable and valuable, and you can only find that by putting the real you out there, being intimate enough to let yourself be hurt. That's the only way to have a worthwhile and successful relationship, whether with a friend, partner or spouse.

The educationalist Sir Ken Robinson added that in order to discover things, gain wisdom and create anything original you have to be prepared to be wrong. I agree. Beware anyone who is too certain about anything, particularly if he is critical of anyone not sharing his belief. The chances are that he's never thought deeply enough or let himself be vulnerable enough to learn anything real from his life. At my most narcissistic I imagine the following rule being named 'Cantopher's law': *The degree of a person's certainty is inversely proportional to his or her wisdom.* Avoid people who are too certain about things. And if you are tempted to retort, 'Ah, but then if you're certain about Cantopher's law, you must be stupid!', then you're a smart alec – refer to the quote at the beginning of this chapter.

We all know people who enjoy humiliating others. The worst are the trolls who heap scorn on others from the safe anonymity of social media and the internet. If someone lobs a packet of poo at you, step aside, don't catch it. Twitter and other social media have a lot of verbal poo. I don't read reviews on Amazon of my books, because, in Dr Brown's words, 'If you're not in the arena failing and getting your ass kicked on a regular basis, I'm not interested in your feedback.' Well, all right, I do a bit, but I'm selective about whose opinions I attend to. I advise you to be very selective about whose opinions you take note of. Take feedback only from those who love and care about you, or those you trust and respect, not those who are habitual critics or who are flatterers either.

Letting yourself fail is the only way I know to survive intact the emotional battering life doles out. Letting others fail is the greatest kindness you can give them. That includes them failing to be good people by your standards, failing to be fair or wise or kind enough. Only tell people what they ask you or what you are fairly confident will help them. Are you sure the 'constructive criticism' you're giving Tania is really meant to help her? Or is it to make yourself feel better, wiser, more powerful? Before you give unsolicited feedback you need to have made a fairly sensitive assessment not just of whether you're right but also of whether the recipient of your words has the fortitude to be able to be helped and not injured by them. Hey, look, none of us is perfect; we can all be irritable and unkind at times. But if that's what's happening, call it what it is and don't pretend that your intention is honourable.

Following this advice may lead you to bottling up some resentments. That doesn't work either. Don't seethe; it isn't good for you. So what to do with your feelings? I think you can use the principles of CBT here (see Chapter 9). Your seething is based on a false assumption: people should be good and fair and like me. Why? Who says the world should only be populated by people you find likeable? Don't blame the bigot for being bigoted, or the bully for bullying. They are who they are and will change only if they choose to. It's *your* job to avoid them or put up effective boundaries against their excesses. As Max Ehrmann says in his beautiful prose poem 'Desiderata': 'Avoid aggressive persons, they are vexatious to the spirit.'

I'm not saying that being a good person doesn't matter. It does, a lot – at least to me. Be as good a person as you can be, to yourself as well as to others. The most powerful way you can do this is by being a kind and compassionate teacher. I'm not contradicting what I said earlier here, about only telling folks what they ask you. But life is about learning, if you choose to, and everything you do and say is a learning experience for you and others who witness it. As I explained early in the book, angry, sadistic, bullying teachers are ineffective at best and can do long-term damage at worst. Warm, encouraging, compassionate, forgiving, interested and persistent teachers are immensely powerful in the good they can do and the wisdom they can generate in their pupils.

So be a good teacher, first to yourself, then also to others as they stumble through life trying to learn from their mistakes and from yours. That's how you develop resilience, not by being tough, cruel or insensitive, but by being gentle and kind to others and to yourself while you're going through the lifelong process of learning. How exciting life can be when there is no fear of failure. Personally, I hate fear. It takes the joy out of whatever you do and it is inefficient. I'm not talking about fear of clear and present danger. If someone is pointing a gun at you, it's a good idea to be afraid. But fear of coming up short, of 'letting myself down', of being criticized by yourself or others? That's just a stultifying waste of time.

There are certain times and situations in which this is both difficult and particularly important. Any public appearance or performance, task at work, effort to gain approval from someone you value, sporting contest the outcome of which matters to you, or effort to help or protect your kids comes into this category. Your best performance comes from really good preparation involving a lot of practice, but then performing *as if the outcome doesn't matter*. The golfer Fred Couples became a better putter by persuading himself that he didn't care whether or not his putt went in the hole, just whether he put a good stroke on the ball. The tennis player Mark Cox, a collaborator in the team that developed the 'Inner Game' approach to sport, discovered that hitting a ball into the vague vicinity of the 'T' on the other side of the net but trying *not* to hit the T itself actually halved the average distance by which the ball missed this mark, compared with actually trying to hit it. So going through the motions, but *not* trying to achieve the desired result, makes it *more* likely you'll do so. Even if you don't reach your goal, treating your failure as information and strength gained makes it more likely you'll get there next time.

So go find some stuff which you might fail at. That's the really worthwhile stuff. Have fun and be generous when you don't win.

If you want to improve your record as a coach, a boss, a leader, a friend or a supportive family member, remember that your most important role is not to urge your subject on to success but to reveal the wonderful power that failure has when treated properly. Resilience comes from reducing the injuries you inflict on yourself and others, the most severe coming from excessive criticism. Focus on kindness and reward, not threats or punishment; on consistency and careful management of change, not change for change's sake; on instilling and operating on mutually held values, not on externally applied injunctions.

And be the 'strong man who stumbles'. As Roosevelt concludes at the end of the quote with which I started this chapter, 'His place shall never be with those cold and timid souls who know neither victory nor defeat.'

Conclusion

OK, I've got a confession to make. You know how in the Introduction I was showing off about how good I am at losing? It isn't entirely true. I thought it was, but my wife pointed out that when she beat me recently at Scrabble, I knocked the board over (oops!) and claimed that there were letters missing. She thinks it's hilarious that I should write a book about how to fail well, as in her opinion I'm about the three hundred millionth best in the USA at that skill. What we're agreed on, though, is that I'm trying to improve and that I'm possibly making a bit of progress with my efforts. When I miss a short putt my oaths are shorter, quieter and slightly less offensive than they were. In any case, you don't want to take your advice from experts who sail unruffled through life without breaking into a sweat, but from the struggling journeyman who is learning from his mistakes. At least, that's what I tell myself.

Whatever my shortcomings, what I try to do is to learn from others who get it right. The best, in my experience, are alcoholics in recovery. Oh, the stories I could tell … but that wouldn't be the point. We've all done stuff we're ashamed of. Addicts, including alcoholics, have done more than most. But many of those who have a good recovery have worked the AA steps of recovery, which give them a degree of self-knowledge and honesty which most of us will never achieve. With these come serenity. Seek out an alcoholic who has made a good recovery and spend some time talking with him or her. You'll see what I mean. If you don't know any, spend time with anyone you meet who has serenity – someone who doesn't fret, resent, bad-mouth people or get angry, but who takes people and life on their own terms. A friend of mine, commenting on some of the challenging characters at our golf club, said to me the other day: 'People are who they are, and it isn't our job to change them.' Spot on.

So while I'm not as good at failing as I'd like to be or as I thought I was, I'm giving it my best shot. I'm learning as I go along. And that's the point, isn't it? You may roll your eyes when I tell you I'm going to talk about the purpose of life, but this is going to be my last book, at least of this genre, and if you can't wax philosophical at the end of your last book then when can you? I'm going to tweak the American Declaration of Independence a tad and tell you that for me life is about love, learning and the pursuit of honesty. At its best, it's about a combination of all three: learning to be more loving of others by learning how to love yourself, despite your shortcomings, and being honest with others as well as yourself because with uncon-ditional love comes the ability to be honest without hurting anyone. So while he died nearly half a century ago, I'm still trying to love the fierce old maths teacher from the Introduction who terrorized me as a child. I believe he was trying to do his best, given very limited emotional resources. I'm a way away from being able to love Donald Trump or his supporters, but I'm trying. Life is a continuing process. You may have your own thoughts about the purposes of your life. If you haven't, then give them some consideration and then pursue them without fear. It's the journey which makes life worthwhile, not the attainment of perfection.

Well, farewell, dear reader. If you've read some of my stuff, I hope it's helped a bit. If not, don't give up. Continue looking for what makes you happy and keeps your head above water through the choppy seas of life. It's out there. Go make a mess of something, forgive yourself, learn from your mistakes and keep looking forward. If you do, I'm confident you'll find what you're seeking, including that most elusive quality of life: joy. I wish you a happy, fun and interesting life, full of failure, success, defeat and victory.

Further reading

This is a list of the books, websites and TV programmes I've mentioned in the text. You don't need to read or watch them all, of course, though they are all well worth the effort.

Books

Bastian, Brock, *The Other Side of Happiness: Embracing a More Fearless Approach to Living*. Penguin, 2018.

Berne, Eric, *Games People Play*. Penguin, 1987.

Brown, Dr Brené, *Daring Greatly*. Penguin, 2012.

Bryson, Bill, *Notes from a Small Island*. William Morrow Paperbacks, 2015.

Burns, David, *The Feeling Good Handbook*, Plume, 1999.

Cantopher, Dr Tim, *Overcoming Anxiety – Without Fighting it*. Sheldon Press, 2019.

Cantopher, Dr Tim, *Toxic People: Dealing with Dysfunctional Relationships*. Sheldon Press, 2017.

Frankl, Dr Viktor, *Man's Search for Meaning*. Beacon Press, 2006.

Hayes, Steven and Smith, Spencer, *Get Out of Your Mind & into Your Life: The New Acceptance and Commitment Therapy*. New Harbinger Publications, 2005.

Kabat-Zinn, Jon, *Wherever You Go, There You Are: Mindfulness Meditation for Everyday Life*. Hyperion, 2004.

Rotella, Dr Bob, *Golf is Not a Game of Perfect*. Simon & Schuster, 2007.

Tolle, Eckhart, *The Power of Now*. New World Library, 2004.

Twenge, Dr Jean, *iGen: Why Today's Super-Connected Kids are Growing Up Less Rebellious, More Tolerant, Less Happy – and Completely Unprepared for Adulthood*. Atria Books, 2017.

Westover, Dr Tara, *Educated*. Random House, 2018.

Williams, Dr Mark and Penman, Danny, *Mindfulness: A Practical Guide to Finding Peace in a Frantic World*. Hachette Digital, 2011.

Websites

CBT

www.moodgym.com.au

Mindfulness apps

www.headspace.com
www.calm.com

Netflix documentary

Brown, Dr Brené, 'The Call to Courage', 2019.

Index

illness related to, 41–5
from major life changes, 72–3
support from friends, 9, 28, 51–2, 66, 73–4
survival, 26
systematic desensitization, 63, 96

talent, 84–5
thinking patterns
  changing, 52–5
  cognitive behavioural therapy (CBT), 11, 58, 94–9
  and depression, 9–13
  and happiness, 31, 67–8
  mindfulness, 12, 53–4, 99–103
time management, 90–2
Tolle, Eckhart, 99–100
toxic people, 14–15, 74–8
trolls, 105
Twenge, Jean, 17–18

value, 25–6, 27–8, 65–6
  judgements, 31–2
variety in life, 27, 28, 64 *see also* change
vitality, 27, 64
vulnerability (*see also* resilience)
  and courage, 104–5
  effect of loss in childhood, 7–8
  effect of stress hormones, 6–7
  learned in childhood, 4–6
  and relationships, 13–15
  vs. resilience, 1–2
  social media, 17–18

Westover, Tara, 36–7
Williams, Mark and Danny Penman, 100
workplace
  clarity, 65
  feelings of powerlessness, 63